D0822105

KNOw
THE ONLY TRUE
GOD

THIS IS ETERNAL LIFE

A 7-Week Bible Study

Suitable for Studying God's Word
Individually or in Small Groups

Corinne Carlson

Light Unto My Path Bible Studies

ISBN 978-0-578-87434-0

Cover photograph StockSnap Pixabay

All Scripture quotations are from the Holy Bible, Authorised King James Version.

Contents

Throughout this study you will see this symbol. It is there to indicate the space that has been provided for you to write down your answers to the questions, the lists suggested, the things the Holy Spirit impresses upon your heart, and even the prayers that flow from your heart as a result of what you studied.

You have heard it many times.
The name of God.

You have heard people who say the name of God as an exclamation of surprise or shock.

You have heard people say, "Lord", too. Many talk about the Lord in times of tragedy or confusing circumstances when man's reasoning seems to fall short of a satisfying explanation.

However, too often the One Who's Name is spoken, God, remains unknown.

Those who call upon His Name do not know Who He is, so they go through life making up their own idea of who God is, often based on their personal experiences.

The result is that many people worship a false god. They worship a god that is not the Only True God as He reveals Himself in His Word.

This is a very sad fact because we have the Word of God in greater availability now than ever before in the history of mankind!

This is all part of the great deception of the prince of this world. He is still doing all he can to change, question or keep us from the Word of God. He knows that the truth will set us free from his bondage, so he works very hard to keep us from It.

> *"The Lord hath a controversy with the inhabitants of the land because there is no truth, nor mercy, nor knowledge of God in the land.....My people are destroyed for lack of knowledge."*
> *Hosea 4: 1 & 6*

Here, then, is where we need to start. Every single one of us. Believer or unbeliever, there is no more important foundation to lay than to know Who God is, and to gain this knowledge from His very own Word, *the Bible*.

> *"And this is life eternal, that they might know Thee the Only True God, and Jesus Christ, Whom Thou hast sent." John 17: 3*

The purpose of this study is:

> *"That the God of our Lord Jesus Christ, the Father of glory, may give unto you the spirit of wisdom and revelation in the knowledge of Him." Ephesians 1: 17*

The results of this study will be:

> *"That we henceforth be no more children, tossed to and fro, and carried about with every wind of doctrine," Ephesians 4: 14a*

and

> *"the people who know their God shall be strong, and do exploits." Daniel 11: 32b*

 **WEEK 1**

"In the Beginning God…"

THE ONLY TRUE

God is Eternal

How do we begin to know God?

Where do we find out about Him? How does He reveal Himself to us, mankind?

God reveals Himself to us in two wonderful ways.

We learn of Him though His creation,

> *"For the invisible things of Him from the creation of the world are clearly seen, being understood by the things that are made, even His eternal power and Godhead;" Romans 1: 20*

And we learn of Him through His Word, *the Bible,*

> *"My son, if thou wilt receive my words, and hide my commandments with thee;*
> *So that thou incline thine ear unto wisdom, and apply thine heart to understanding;*
> *Yea, if thou criest after knowledge, and liftest up thy voice for understanding;*
> *If thou seekest her as silver, and searchest for her as for hid treasures;*
> *Then shalt thou understand the fear of the LORD, and find the knowledge of God." Proverbs 2: 1-5*

Think about how you are alive for a moment.

You are alive and doing this study because your heart is beating somewhere between 60 and 80 times per minute, continually replenishing every cell in your body with the fresh oxygen needed to function. You are alive because you are breathing about 16 to 20 times per minute without having to tell yourself to, and this supplies your heart with freshly oxygenated blood to pump to every cell in your body with each one of its beats.

There is nothing you can do to keep this going, to keep yourself alive.

It is God who keeps your heart beating. And it is God who causes your brain to continually send signals for you to take a breath!

No one has ever been able to create life out of innate items.

We can understand how it all happens, but we cannot give the breath of life when it has stopped or when it was never there to begin with.

This is one example of how God reveals Himself through His creation to the heart that is willing to know Him.

Since man had to be given life to exist, God already had to be in existence.

Think about that as we begin this study of His Word, *the Bible*, to find out how He reveals Himself there.

 DAY 1

Always begin your study of God's Word with prayer. Ask God to open the eyes of your understanding.

Read the following verses through once.

Then read them again out loud.

Read them a 3rd time, while marking each reference to **God**, including pronouns, with a blue triangle, like this:

Genesis 1: 1, 2, 26

> **1** In the beginning God created the heaven and the earth.
>
> **2** And the earth was without form, and void; and darkness was upon the face of the deep.
>
> And the Spirit of God moved upon the face of the waters.
>
> ...
>
> **26** And God said, Let Us make man in Our image, after Our likeness: and let them have dominion over the fish of the sea, and over the fowl of the air, and over the cattle, and over all the earth, and over every creeping thing that creepeth upon the earth.

Marking key words helps you to observe more carefully what God's Word is saying. You will be doing this throughout this study keeping the same color code for each key word that you mark.

Another important thing to notice and mark is time. Underline every reference to time with a yellow line. It will be any phrase or word that answers the question, "when?".

What did you learn from marking the references to God in these verses?

When did this take place?

What did God do?

Who are the main characters mentioned in these verses?

What did God have, to start with?

Was anyone present besides God?

Did you notice the pronouns God uses in verse 26, in what He says? If you didn't, mark them with your triangle now. How does God refer to Himself with these pronouns?

The Bible is the very Word of God. The first chapter of Genesis, which is the first book of *the Bible*, is where God introduces Himself to us.

From this very first chapter, we learn that He was there before anything else ever existed, and we learn that He is just as He made us: more than one part. We saw in verse two, that a part of Him is His Spirit. Tomorrow we will see Who is another part of the God of *the Bible*.

As you end your study time today, ask God to help you see how He reveals Himself to you through His creation. Ask Him also to increase your faith so

> *"That the God of our Lord Jesus Christ, the Father of glory, may give unto you the spirit of wisdom and revelation in the knowledge of Him." Ephesians 1: 17*

 DAY 2

Begin with prayer, asking God to

"Open Thou mine eyes, that I might behold wondrous things out of Thy law." Psalm 119: 17

Yesterday you marked the pronouns **Us** and **Our** in Genesis 1: 26, referring to God. You saw in Genesis 1:2 that ***"the Spirit of God moved upon the face of the waters;"*** therefore, we can see that the pronouns Us and Our refer to God and His Spirit.

There is a third person that is part of Who God is, Who was there also in the beginning.

Read the following verses three times; one of these times out loud. On your third reading mark every reference to **God** with your blue triangle.

John 1: 1-4, 14-18

1 In the beginning was the Word, and the Word was with God, and the Word was God.

2 The same was in the beginning with God.

3 All things were made by Him; and without Him was not anything made that was made.

4 In Him was life: and the life was the Light of men.

...

14 And the Word was made flesh, and dwelt among us, (and we beheld His glory, the glory as of the only begotten of the Father,) full of grace and truth.

15 John bare witness of Him, and cried, saying, This was He of Whom I spake, He that cometh after me is preferred before me: for He was before me.

16 And of His fulness have all we received, and grace for grace.

17 For the law was given by Moses, but grace and truth came by Jesus Christ.

18 No man hath seen God at any time: the only begotten Son, which is in the bosom of the Father, He hath declared Him.

Now mark every reference to *the Word*, including pronouns and synonyms, with a blue triangle that has a cross in it:

Continue observing the text you read by underlining every reference to time with a yellow line, such as *beginning, after, before*.

Looking at your markings make a list of what the text tells you about each reference to *the Word*. Keep your list to just what the text tells you. It is important not to add your own thoughts or interpretation. We will move to that after we have carefully examined the text.

Your list should look like this: (It is started for you, continue adding to the list as you move verse by verse. This may seem tedious, but you will begin to see God showing you things you didn't see at first. Be faithful, you will be rewarded!)

The Word:
v. 1 was in the beginning
    was with God
    was God
v. 2 was in the beginning
    was with God
v. 3

In verse 15, what does John say about the Word?

Read verses 17-18 again. What is the Word's name? How is He described in verse 18?

Did you notice the reference to time? *In the beginning*. Did you notice that it refers to the same time that Genesis 1:1 refers to? Where was the Word in the beginning, when God created the heavens and the earth?

How does what we just studied fit in with what we saw yesterday in Genesis? Does this show us Who the *Us* and *Our* refer to in Genesis 1: 26?

From what you have studied so far, list the Three Persons that make up the One True God of the Bible:

📅 DAY 3

Begin with asking God to show Himself to you as you study His Word today.

Today, let's look at a passage of God's Word where we see what God the Father says about His Son.

Read the passage three times again, one of those times read it out loud, and the last time you read it, mark every reference to the Son with a blue triangle with a cross in it. Mark all the pronouns and synonyms as well.

Hebrews 1: 8-12

8 But unto the Son He saith, Thy throne, O God, is for ever and ever: a sceptre of righteousness is the sceptre of Thy kingdom.

9 Thou hast loved righteousness, and hated iniquity: therefore God, even Thy God, hath anointed Thee with the oil of gladness above Thy fellows.

10 And, Thou, LORD, in the beginning hast laid the foundations of the earth; and the heavens are the work of Thy hands:

11 They shall perish; but Thou remainest; and they shall wax old as doth a garment;

12 And as a vesture shalt Thou fold them up, and they shall be changed: but Thou art the same, and Thy years shall not fail.

Now, using your markings, make your list about the Son. List everything God tells you about the Son. It is started below for you:

The Son:
v. 8 He has a throne
  His throne is eternal
  He is God
  He has a kingdom
v. 9

Did you notice the references to time in these verses? One of them is the same phrase we read in the previous two passages we studied.

There are three references to time in these verses. Locate them and underline them with a yellow line, as you did before. They are in verses 8, 10 and 12.

In the beginning, the key phrase you underlined in the three passages we have studied so far, tells us so much.

Answer the following questions with the words of God's Word as much as possible. Stick to what the text tells us, avoid interpretation for now.

What role did the Son of God have in the beginning?

What do these references to time tell you about God?

Who was there in the beginning? (Answer this based on all three passages we have studied.)

Were God, His Son, and the Spirit of God part of what was created in the beginning?

As you end your time of study today, think about the significance of what you have observed for yourself in *the Bible*, the Word of God, about Who God is. Tell God what this means to you, and ask Him to help you align what you believe about Him with what He reveals about Himself in His Word.

Many times as we study God's Word, God shows us important truths, and it really does feel like He opens the eyes of our understanding. Some have called these Life Lessons. When God gives you one of those, be sure to write it down in this study guide; blank spaces are intentionally left for that purpose. You will want to be able to go back often and reread what God showed you, and you will be able to share that with those whom God puts in your life to encourage, teach or minister to.

 DAY 4

Start out by asking the Lord for His help as you study to learn Who He is.

As you study God's Word and as you progress through each day's instructions and answer each question in this guide, don't be discouraged or frustrated if you come to a point where you just don't know. There are no right or wrong answers. This is not a course with a pass or fail grade at the end. If you don't know an answer, just stop and ask God to show you what He wants you to see and learn. He is your Teacher, and He knows exactly what He wants you to learn. He will show Himself to you.

Today, we are going to look at another passage of God's Word that tells us more about the Son of God, Jesus-Christ.

Read the passage below as you have the previous passages. Read it three times; one of those times read it out loud, and on the last reading, mark each reference to **God** with a blue triangle, and each reference to God's dear Son, *Jesus*, with a blue triangle with a cross inside.

Colossians 1: 13-16

13 Who *[God]* hath delivered us from the power of darkness, and hath translated us into the kingdom of His dear Son:

14 In Whom we have redemption through His blood, even the forgiveness of sins:

15 Who is the image of the invisible God, the firstborn of every creature:

16 For by Him were all things created, that are in heaven, and that are in earth, visible and invisible, whether they be thrones, or dominions, or principalities, or powers: all things were created by Him and for Him:

Now, make a list of all that you learn from marking the references to the Son. Again the list is started to help you.

The Son:
v. *13 He has a kingdom*
   He is dear

Look again at verse 16. What part did the Son have in the creation account of Genesis 1?

What can the Son do for mankind? On what basis?

According to verse 16, why was man created?

Think about that. What does that mean to you personally?

You just read that all things were created through Jesus Christ. What were they created out of? Did anything exist before creation?

Before we conclude today's study, let's look at one more verse.

Hebrews 13: 8

Jesus-Christ the same yesterday, today and for ever.

What does that verse tell you about Jesus Christ, the Son? Was there a time He did not exist?

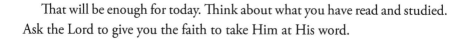

That will be enough for today. Think about what you have read and studied. Ask the Lord to give you the faith to take Him at His word.

📅 DAY 5

Begin your study with prayer and ask God to renew your mind.
Pray Romans 12: 2

> *"And be not conformed to this world: but be transformed by the*
> *renewing of your mind, that ye may prove what is that good, and*
> *acceptable, and perfect, will of God."*

Read the verses below three times; one of these times being out loud. With
the last reading, mark every references to **God,** including the pronouns that
refer to Him, with a blue triangle.

Psalm 90: 1-2

1 LORD, Thou hast been our dwelling place in all generations.
2 Before the mountains were brought forth, or ever Thou hadst formed
the earth and the world, even from everlasting to everlasting Thou art
God.

Hebrews 11: 1-3, 6

1 Now faith is the substance of things hoped for, the evidence of things
not seen.
2 For by it the elders obtained a good report.
3 Through faith we understand that the worlds were framed by the
Word of God, so that things which are seen are not made of things
which do appear.
...
6 But without faith it is impossible to please Him: for he that cometh
to God must believe that He is, and that He is a rewarder of them that
diligently seek Him.

Now choose a different color and draw a box around the words **brought forth, formed, framed, made.**

Mark the word **faith** with a green F.

What do you learn about God in Psalm 90?

What did you learn from marking *brought forth, formed, framed, made* in these two passages?

What did God use to create everything He made?

What existed before the worlds were made?

How do you know this?

Make a list of what you learn in these verses about faith.

Faith:

v. 1

How does what you learn about faith apply to your understanding of God?

Think about the many things people believe about God. What are you going to believe about God and on what are you going to base your belief?

"For ever, O LORD, Thy Word is settled in heaven." Psalm 119: 89

"I will worship toward Thy holy temple, and praise Thy Name for Thy lovingkindness and for Thy truth: for Thou hast magnified Thy Word above all Thy Name." Psalm 138: 2

Think about what God has shown you about Himself so far and

"choose you this day Whom you will serve" Joshua 24: 15a

📅 DAY 6

So far God has revealed to us in His Word that He was there in the beginning and that He created everything we know out of nothing. He simply spoke everything into existence. He is self-existent.

He did not need to be created. He has no beginning, and there is nothing He needs apart from Himself. He is self-sufficient.

He is God *"from everlasting to everlasting"* (Psalm 90: 2). He is eternal.

Before we go any further, ask the Lord to help you as you study His Word today.

Let's look at how He reveals Himself to Moses, in Exodus 3, and then how Moses describes Him in his blessing of the children of Israel before his death in Deuteronomy 33.

Exodus 3: 13-15

13 And Moses said unto God, Behold, when I come unto the children of Israel, and shall say unto them, The God of your fathers hath sent me unto you; and they shall say to me, What is his name? What shall I say unto them?
14 And God said unto Moses, I AM THAT I AM: and He said, Thus shalt thou say unto the children of Israel, I AM hath sent me unto you.
15 And God said moreover unto Moses, Thus shalt thou say unto the children of Israel, The LORD God of your fathers, the God of Abraham, the God of Isaac, and the God of Jacob, hath sent me unto you: this is My Name for ever, and this is My memorial unto all generations.

Deuteronomy 33: 27

27 The eternal God is thy refuge, and underneath are the everlasting arms: and He shall thrust out the enemy from before thee; and shall say, Destroy them.

Read these verses through twice again; once out loud. Mark every reference to **God** with your blue triangle. Be careful not to miss any of the pronouns that refer to Him.

Now make a list of all the ways that God identifies Himself to Moses, to you and to me in these verses.

God:
Exodus 3 v. 13 the God of Moses's fathers
       v. 14

Did you see the references to time in verse Exodus 3: 15 and in Deuteronomy 33: 27? What does it tell us?

I AM is YHWH (Yaweh, or Jehovah) in Hebrew. It comes from the word which means to exist or be. God calls this Name, by which He reveals Himself to Moses, His memorial Name. For whom is this Name to be a memorial?

"For of Him, and through Him, and to Him, are all things: to Whom be glory for ever. Amen." Romans 11: 36

In Him is everything and anything we will ever need!
God is self-existent, self-sufficient, eternal!
And He wants us to know Him! Do you begin to see how He wants a relationship with you?

 **DAY 7**

Begin with prayer. Ask God to help you see Who He is and know Him.

Let's conclude this week's study on God's eternal existence by looking at what He tells us in Revelation, the last book in His Word.

Read through the following verses three times; one of which is read aloud. By now you have noticed what reading out loud does: it helps see details and things that can be missed in a silent reading. Mark every reference to ***God***, including pronouns and synonyms, with a blue triangle. Mark the references to ***Jesus Christ*** with a blue triangle with a cross in it.

Revelation 1: 8, 17-18

8 I am Alpha and Omega, the beginning and the ending, saith the Lord, which is, and which was, and which is to come, the Almighty.

. . .

17 And when I saw Him, I fell at His feet as dead. And He laid His right hand upon me, saying unto me, Fear not; I am the first and the last:

18 I am He that liveth, and was dead; and, behold, I am alive for evermore, Amen; and have the keys of hell and of death.

Revelation 4: 2, 9

2 And immediately I was in the spirit: and, behold, a throne was set in heaven, and One sat on the throne.

. . .

9 And when those beasts give glory and honor and thanks to Him that sat on the throne, Who liveth for ever and ever,

What do you learn from marking the references to God?

According to Revelation 1: 18, and Revelation 2: 9, how long will God be alive?

Do you believe God is eternal? That He had no beginning and will have no end? Why?

If you truly believe that God, His Son Jesus Christ and His Spirit have always existed, how does that impact your life? What difference does it make to know this about God?

If you are staring at the blank page, not knowing what to answer, remember, ask God to show you…and humbly wait, while you reread the words He spoke to You in his Word. He will show you.

The Everlasting, Eternal God wants to reveal Himself to you through the pages of His Word.

We are only beginning to know the Only True God.

To worship is to look at someone's worth and to bow before him in reverence.

Is He worthy of your worship yet?

"For thus saith the high and lofty One that inhabiteth eternity, whose name is Holy; I dwell in the high and holy place, with him also that is of a contrite and humble spirit, to revive the spirit of the humble, and to revive the heart of the contrite ones."
Isaiah 57: 15

📅 **WEEK 2**

THE ONLY TRUE

God is the Creator of All

The Only True God is eternal.

He has no beginning and no end. By faith we accept that He is infinite; He has always been.

The more we study to know Him as He reveals Himself to us in His Word, *the Bible*, the more we see how little we know and how limited we are.

Yet, we also begin to see and marvel at the realization that He wants us to know Him and He wants to be our God!

How is this possible?

It begins with the fact that He created us. This is what we are going to study this week. God is our Creator, and He is the Creator of all.

📅 DAY 1

Begin by asking the Lord for His help as you study. Pray Colossians 1: 10:

> *"That ye might walk worthy of the Lord unto all pleasing, being fruitful in every good work, and increasing in the knowledge of God;"*

Read the text of the Word of God below three times, one of these times reading it out loud. On the third reading mark every reference to **God** with a blue triangle as you have been doing, including the pronouns and synonyms.

Genesis1: 1-5

1 In the beginning God created the heaven and the earth.
2 And the earth was without form, and void;
and darkness was upon the face of the deep.
And the Spirit of God moved upon the face of the waters.
3 And God said, Let there be light: and there was light.
4 And God saw the light, that it was good:
and God divided the light from the darkness.
5 And God called the light Day, and the darkness he called Night.
And the evening and the morning were the first day.

Now, go back over the text and underline the phrase **God said** with a wavy blue line.

Then circle the word, ***day,*** with a yellow circle every time you see it.

Underline each phrase that refers to time with a yellow line.

What do you see that God does in these five verses? List each of His actions.

How did God do each of these actions? If you aren't sure how to answer this question, look up Psalm 33: 6.

How many days are described in this passage?

How is a day defined?

Read the entire chapter of Genesis 1 in your own Bible, and see what God creates on each of the days that follow. Then list below what He creates on each day:

Day 1:

Day 2:

Day 3:

Day 4:

Day 5:

Day 6:

Now, read this next passage, again three times, once out loud, and mark every reference to *the LORD* with a blue triangle.

Psalm 136: 1, 5-9

1 O give thanks unto the LORD; for He is good: for His mercy endureth for ever.

...

5 To Him that by wisdom made the heavens: for His mercy endureth for ever.

6 To Him that stretched out the earth above the waters: for His mercy endureth for ever.

7 To Him that made great lights: for His mercy endureth for ever.

8 The sun to rule by day: for His mercy endureth for ever.

9 The moon and stars to rule by night: for His mercy endureth for ever.

This is a song of praise and gratitude to God for His mercy.

According to verse one why should we give thanks unto the LORD?

According to verse five how did He make the heavens?

The Hebrew word used here, and translated *mercy*, means *kindness*. Think about that, and list below what shows God's kindness in each of the verses you just read. Write down why each item shows His kindness. Again, don't worry about "the right answer". The right answer is the one the Holy Spirit shows you.

Evidences of God's kindness:

Think about what you have seen today. Did it fill your heart with gratefulness for God's great wisdom in His work of creation?

Talk to the Lord about how this applies to your daily life.

There are times when writing out our prayer to the Lord helps us to express ourselves better. You can use the space provided here to write what you want to say to the Lord.

📅 DAY 2

Begin with prayer. Pray Ephesians 1: 17,

> *"That the God of our Lord Jesus Christ, the Father of glory, may give unto you the spirit of wisdom and revelation in the knowledge of Him:"*

Yesterday, we looked at the account of how God created the heavens and the earth. Today, let's look at His work of creation from His perspective.

We can see that in an answer He gives to Job.

Job was a man who lived in the very early days following creation, and he is described by God Himself as perfect and upright. He lived in the fear and respect of God, and because of that, Satan, the devil, challenged God that Job only feared Him because of all that God did for him. As a result, God gave Satan permission to strip Job of all that he enjoyed except life itself.

Job suffered incredibly, and yet, he never gave up on God. Instead, this is what he said:

> *"Naked came I out of my mother's womb, and naked shall I return thither: the LORD gave, and the LORD hath taken away: blessed be the Name of the LORD." Job 1: 21*

Satan challenged God again by saying that as long as he had his own life, Job was fearing God just to preserve his life. So, God allowed Satan to destroy his health but keep him alive. Again, Job stayed true and faithful to God. When even his wife encouraged him to curse God and die, he said this to her:

> *"What? Shall we receive good at the hand of God, and shall we not receive evil?" Job 2: 10*

Later, when he was suffering greatly from his physical illness, some of his friends thought he must have done something wrong to deserve all this. This is what Job said to them:

> *"Though He slay me, yet will I trust in Him: but I will maintain mine own ways before Him." Job 13: 15*

After his friends had said all they knew to say to him, Job began to ask God why; he rehearsed all the good that he had done and all the right choices that he had made in his life and asked God why was He not rewarding him for all of his righteousness.

God then answered Job, and in His answer we see creation from God's viewpoint.

Read this portion of God's Word three times; one of those times read it out loud, and continue to mark every reference to **God** with a blue triangle.

Job 38: 1-6, 12, 18-29, 35-36

1 Then the LORD answered Job out of the whirlwind, and said,

2 Who is this that darkeneth counsel by words without knowledge?

3 Gird up now thy loins like a man; for I will demand of thee, and answer thou Me.

4 Where wast thou when I laid the foundations of the earth? declare, if thou hast understanding.

5 Who hath laid the measures thereof, if thou knowest? or who hath stretched the line upon it?

6 Whereupon are the foundations thereof fastened? or who laid the corner stone thereof;

...

12 Hast thou commanded the morning since thy days; and caused the dayspring to know his place;

...

18 Hast thou perceived the breadth of the earth? declare if thou knowest it all.

19 Where is the way where light dwelleth? and as for darkness, where is the place thereof,

20 That thou shouldest take it to the bound thereof, and that thou shouldest know the path to the house thereof?

21 Knowest thou it, because thou wast then born? or because the number of thy days is great?

22 Hast thou entered into the treasures of the snow? or hast thou seen the treasures of the hail,

23 Which I have reserved against the time of trouble, against the day of battle and war?

24 By what way is the light parted, which scattereth the east wind upon the earth?

25 Who hath divided a watercourse for the overflowing of waters, or a way for the lightning of thunder;

26 To cause it to rain on the earth, where no man is; on the wilderness, wherein there is no man;

27 To satisfy the desolate and waste ground; and to cause the bud of the tender herb to spring forth?

28 Hath the rain a father? or who hath begotten the drops of dew?

29 Out of who's womb came the ice? and the hoary frost of heaven, who hath gendered it?

...

35 Canst thou send lightnings, that they may go, and say unto thee, Here we are?

36 Who hath put wisdom in the inward parts? or who hath given understanding to the heart?

These verses, which are only a portion of what God said to Job, give us much to think about.

Mark every reference to *earth* with a brown circle including every pronoun.

Mark every reference to *light* by highlighting them in yellow including the pronouns.

List below what you learn about the creation of the earth from marking it. Keep it simple; just list what the verse tells you about it.

Earth:
v. 4 it has foundations
v. 5 it has measures

Now list everything you learn about light.
Light:

Underline every reference to weather processes in these verses with a wavy purple line, and list them below:

Think about it: can man make rain? Hail? Thunder? Lightning? Wind? Snow? Frost? Dew?

Those of us who enjoy skiing know that ski resorts have figured out how to "make snow", but we also know that it has no comparison with real snow! Man-made snow is really just frozen water and it is not very good to ski on.

God is the Creator of real snow, just as He is the Creator of all of the weather patterns we try our best to analyze and forecast.

Did you notice also, in verse 12, God's question to Job? Have you ever thought about that?

Who tells the morning to get up?

God's answer to Job gives us His perspective on creation, and it also gives us a better understanding about ourselves in relationship to how powerful, infinite, and amazing God is.

How do the truths you studied today impact you?

Is there anything you need to change in what you believe?

Is there anything you need to change in how you relate to God? Write it all down and then be sure to talk to Him about it.

 # DAY 3

Begin with prayer. Ask God to

"guide you into all truth" John 16: 13

The better we understand how God created man, the better we will understand our purpose. The more we know about God's creation of man, the more we will see His design.

Read the following passages three times; one of which is out loud. Mark all the references to **God** as you have been doing with your blue triangle.

Genesis 1:26-28, 31; 2: 1,7; 5: 1-2

26 And God said, Let Us make man in Our image, after Our likeness: and let them have dominion over the fish of the sea, and over the fowl of the air, and over the cattle, and over all the earth, and over every creeping thing that creepeth upon the earth.

27 So God created man in His own image, in the image of God created He him; male and female created He them.

28 And God blessed them , and God said unto them, Be fruitful, and multiply, and replenish the earth, and subdue it: and have dominion over the fish of the sea, and over the fowl of the air, and over every living thing that moveth upon the earth.

…

31 And God saw everything that He had made, and, behold, it was very good. And the evening and the morning were the sixth day.

2: 1 Thus the heavens and the earth were finished, and all the host of them.

…

2: 7 And the LORD God formed man of the dust of the ground, and breathed into his nostrils the breath of life; and man became a living soul.

…

5: 1 This is the book of the generations of Adam. In the day that God created man, in the likeness of God made He him;

2 Male and female created He them; and blessed them, and called their name Adam, in the day when they were created.

Whenever God repeats a word or phrase several times in His Word, we can be sure that He is pointing us to a key concept that He wants us to see. That is why we are marking key words and paying close attention to what we are learning from them.

Using a different color, draw a box around every reference to **man** including the pronouns.

Circle the word, **day**, in yellow, and underline every reference to time with a yellow line.

Underline the phrase, **God said**, with a wavy blue line.

From marking **God** in this passage, you can see six verbs that describe what He does.

List below what you see God do in theses verses:

How did God create man? There are three characteristics in these verses that describe how God created man.

Go back over Genesis 1 in your Bible, and look at how God created the animals. What is different about how God created the animals and how He created man?

What instructions does God give to man in verse 28?

What does God want man's relationship to the animals to be?

When did the creation of man happen?

How does what you believe about the creation of man compare to what we have just studied?

God reveals Himself to us as our Creator right from the very first chapter of His Word.

Think about this. There are more scriptures in which God tells us about how He created man. We will look at those tomorrow.

▣ DAY 4

Ask the Lord to help you to seek Him as you study His Word today. Ask Him to keep your thoughts focused and to help you

"Be still, and know that I am God:" Psalm 46: 10a

Read the passages below three times; once out loud.

Psalm 139: 13-16

13 For Thou hast possessed my reins: Thou hast covered me in my mother's womb.
14 I will praise Thee; for I am fearfully and wonderfully made: marvelous are Thy works; and that my soul knoweth right well.
15 My substance was not hid from Thee, when I was made in secret, and curiously wrought in the lowest parts of the earth.
16 Thine eyes did see my substance, yet being unperfect; and in Thy book all my members were written, which in continuance were fashioned, when as yet there was none of them.

Exodus 4: 10-12

10 And Moses said unto the LORD, O my Lord, I am not eloquent, neither heretofore, nor since Thou hast spoken unto Thy servant: but I am slow of speech, and of a slow tongue.
11 And the LORD said unto him, Who hath made man's mouth? Or Who maketh the dumb, or deaf, or the seeing, or the blind? have not I the LORD?
12 Now therefore go, and I will be with thy mouth, and teach thee what thou shalt say.

Psalm 100: 3

3 Know ye that the LORD He is God: it is He that hath made us, and not we ourselves; we are His people, and the sheep of His pasture.

Mark every reference to **God**, including the pronouns, with the same blue triangle you have been using.

Mark every reference to **made, wrought, fashioned** in the same color you chose for this key word last week on day five.

There are two references to time in these verses, and you will notice them by looking for the word, **when**. Underline with a yellow line the phrases that start with **when**.

What do you learn about God in these passages? Look at each blue triangle marking and write down what each reference tells us about Him.

List everything that God made, from marking the references to God in these verses.

How does the Psalmist describe that he was made?

Where was he made?

What do you learn from underlining the phrases that started with *when*?

Isn't it amazing to learn that God sees us as we are being formed in our mother's womb? Isn't it even more amazing that He knew everything about every part of us well before we were formed?

Did you ever think about how fearfully and wonderfully you are made? We usually don't even think about that until something goes wrong and we have to go see a Doctor…then we find out, little by little, how intricately and amazingly our bodies function!

What is the Psalmist's response to this realization?

If you believe the truths you have studied today, how do these truths impact your life?

God created man. Male and female created He them. He did it intentionally, purposefully, for a reason.

God created you. He created me.

He created each one of us exactly the way He wants us to be. He clearly planned it all out precisely, well before we were ever born or even conceived. None of us is an "accident" or a mistake.

Do you accept by faith that you have been created by God just the way you are because that's how He planned for you to be?

Will you praise Him by accepting His design for you?

Talk to Him about it, and write out what God speaks to your heart.

Tomorrow we will study scriptures in which God reveals to us why He created us, what His plan was. Nothing is more fulfilling than to understand why we exist and what is our purpose for living.

> *"For thus saith the LORD that created the heavens: God Himself that formed the earth and made it; He hath established it, He created it not in vain, He formed it to be inhabited: I am the LORD; and there is none else." Isaiah 45: 18*

📅 DAY 5

Begin your study of God's Word with prayer.

We have now seen from His Word that the Only True God is eternal, and that He created the heavens and the earth. He created us, mankind. In our studying, we have seen that His work of creation was precisely planned and organized. He had a plan in everything that He did. Does He share His plan with us?

Read the Scriptures below three times; one of those times aloud. While you read, mark every reference to **God** with a blue triangle, and every reference to His **Son** Jesus-Christ with a blue cross inside a triangle including the pronouns.

Isaiah 43: 1, 3-4, 7

1 But now thus saith the LORD that created thee, O Jacob, and He that formed thee, O Israel, Fear not:

…

3 For I am the LORD thy God,

…

4 Since thou wast precious in my sight, thou hast been honourable, and I have loved thee:

…

7 Even everyone that is called by my Name: for I have created him for my glory, I have formed him; yea, I have made him.

Ephesians 2: 10

For we are His workmanship, created in Christ Jesus unto good works, which God hath before ordained that we should walk in them.

Colossians 1: 13-16

13 Who hath delivered us from the power of darkness, and hath

translated us into the kingdom of His dear Son:

14 In Whom we have redemption through His blood, even the forgiveness of sins:

15 Who is the image of the invisible God, the firstborn of every creature:

16 For by Him were all things created, that are in heaven, and that are in earth, visible and invisible, whether they be thrones, or dominions, or principalities, or powers: all things were created by Him and for Him:

Mark every reference to the key words *created* and *formed* the same way you marked *made* yesterday.

Make a list of what you learn from marking the references to God.

Make a list of everything you learn from marking the *Son*, Jesus Christ.

Another useful tool in studying God's word is to notice and mark words that communicate a conclusion. Those are usually words that answer the question why. Often, they are "therefore" or "for".

For example, in Isaiah 43:3, we see "For I am the LORD thy God". This answers a why question: you see that by looking at verse 2: "Fear not". Why should we not fear? Because God is the LORD our God.

According to the verses you read today, why was man created?

Why were you created?

The Hebrew word for glory is *kabod*, which means *"splendor, copiousness"*. Think about that for a moment.

God created us for His glory. For His splendor. For His copiousness…

Think: He created us so that His majestic splendor, abundance, generosity would be what we reflect through our lives!

Is this how you live each day that He gives you? Do you live your life in such a way that you reflect the splendor and copiousness of God? Does your life cause others to catch a glimpse of God's splendor and copiousness?

Think about your attitudes, your choices, you reactions to what happens in your life, wanted and unwanted. Do you need to realign yourself with the truths you have seen today?

Answer these questions as if you were standing before the Only True God, the One Who formed you, Who loves you and Who wants to be your God.

"For God, Who commanded the light to shine out of darkness, hath shined in our hearts, to give the light of the knowledge of the glory of God in the face of Jesus Christ." 2 Corinthians 4: 6

 DAY 6

Begin your study by asking God to protect your mind from distractions and to help you see the truth by which He wants to set you free.

> *"Then said Jesus to those Jews which believed on Him, If ye*
> *continue in My Word, then ye are My disciples indeed;*
> *And ye shall know the truth, and the truth shall make you free."*
> *John 8: 31-32*

In Genesis 1 we see God create the heavens and the earth and everything in them. Throughout the chapter we see God create, then He sees that what He created was good. Then in Genesis 2, God goes into a little more detail about His creation, and we read more about His creation of man. We read about the beginning of His relationship with man. We see how He provides a place for man to live, and how He gives man his first job: to dress and keep the garden of Eden. Work is not a curse; it is actually a gift from God!

However, in Genesis 2: 18, we see for the first time that God finds something that is not good. What He does next is a very important part of His creation. God creates marriage!

Read the following verses three times; one of those times read them out loud. Continue with marking every reference to *God* with a blue triangle.

Genesis 2: 18-25

18 And the LORD God said, It is not good that the man should be alone: I will make him an help meet for him.
19 And out of the ground the LORD God formed every beast of the field, and every foul of the air; and brought them unto Adam to see what he would call them: and whatsoever Adam called every living creature, that was the name thereof.
20 And Adam gave names to all cattle, and to the fowl of the air, and to every beast of the field; but for Adam there was not found an help meet for him.

21 And the LORD God caused a deep sleep to fall upon Adam, and he slept: and He took one of his ribs, and closed up the flesh instead thereof;

22 And the rib, which the LORD God had taken from man, made He a woman, and brought her unto the man.

23 And Adam said, This is now bone of my bones, and flesh of my flesh: she shall be called Woman, because she was taken out of Man.

24 Therefore shall a man leave his father and his mother, and shall cleave unto his wife, and they shall be one flesh.

25 And they were both naked, the man and his wife, and were not ashamed.

This is a beautiful passage of Scripture! It is a good thing to think long and deep about all that God reveals to us in theses verses.

In Genesis 1 we saw that God created man male and female. In Genesis 2 we see what that means; we see how He made man in two specific genders, male and female. We see the creation of woman; we see why He created woman; and again, we see that God does everything with a plan, a purpose.

We see many **FIRSTS** in these verses:
- the first anesthesia, "a deep sleep"
- the first surgery, "He took one of his ribs, and closed up the flesh thereof"
- the first wedding, "and brought her unto the man"
- the first marriage, "Therefore shall a man leave his father and mother, and shall cleave unto his wife, and they shall be one flesh."

Make a list below of what God teaches you about Himself in these verses. Try to stay as close to what the text tells you as possible.

Now, go back through the passage and mark every reference to **man**, including Adam (which means *the man*) in the same way you marked it before. Also, mark the word **made** in the same way you did before.

What did God say was not good?

What did He decide to do about that?

What is the conclusion at the end of verse 20 when Adam has named all the animals?

Think about that. Why do you think that there was not found an help meet for him?

Why does Adam say what he does when God brings him his help meet for him, woman? What was different special to him about her?

The Hebrew words help meet are *ezer neged*. *Ezer* means *aid,* and *neged* means *counterpart* or *part opposite*. This is is what is unique about what woman is to man: she is the counterpart that helps him be whole! A man without a wife is missing his part opposite, his counterpart. Because of that, he is not whole, and he doesn't function as well. A wife completes her man enabling him to be all that God created him to be. Furthermore, in being that counterpart, that completer, she finds her fulfillment and worth!

Oh, it's not what we hear or see in our society, and many have rebelled against this truth thinking that a woman should be equal to a man, free to do and be everything a man does and is. God designed woman with her own excellent purpose and worth! He did not create her to be less than man in any way. Sadly, in the pursuit of what our society calls equality, women have lost much; women have lost the joy and fulfillment that comes from being who God designed them to be. God did not create man male and female so that they would compete and rival each other. God created man male and female to be equal in worth and value yet different in design and purpose!

In verse 24 we see a term of conclusion, "therefore". What is it there for? What is the conclusion God gives? There had not ever been a father or a mother yet.

Genesis 2: 24 is the definition of the relationship God created, that we call marriage. A man leaves his father and mother, cleaves to his wife, and they become one flesh. Becoming one flesh means becoming one unit, one family, a whole. A man and his wife are designed by God to be a completed unit. A man and his wife fit together like no other pair. Anatomy, physiology, emotions and every aspect of how we are made verify and confirm the perfection of God's design and plan.

Sin has corrupted God's design and plan, but that does not mean that God made a mistake or that His plan doesn't work. Satan has been hard at work to destroy what God created. He does all he can to convince us that God is at fault for the failures and suffering that we experience in marriage. So we are in constant search of happiness in marriage. Redefining marriage apart from God's perfect design is a choice that will not lead to that happiness.

"All we like sheep have gone astray; we have turned every one to his own way;" Isaiah 53: 6a

God loves us. He does not force us to follow His plan. If we study to understand His plan, we have a choice: we can choose by faith to live according to the plan He designed for us; or we can choose to do what we think is best for us. Choosing God's plan leads us to finding that joy and happiness we so desperately long for. Making that choice requires knowing and understanding God's design.

"My people are destroyed for lack of knowledge." Hosea 4: 6

When we study God's Word, it is helpful to look at parallel passages. Many times that gives more understanding on what God is telling us. The Bible is always its own best commentary. Read the parallel passage below about the creation of marriage three times; one of those times being out loud. Mark every reference to **God** with the blue triangle and every reference to ***Jesus*** with a blue triangle and a cross inside.

Mark 10: 2-9

2 And the Pharisees came to Him, and asked Him, Is it lawful for a man to put away his wife? tempting Him.

3 And He answered and said unto them, What did Moses command you?

4 And they said, Moses suffered to write a bill of divorcement, and to put her away.

5 And Jesus answered and said unto them, For the hardness of your heart he wrote you this precept.

6 But from the beginning of the creation God made them male and female.

7 For this cause shall a man leave his father and mother, and cleave to his wife;

8 And they twain shall be one flesh: so then they are no more twain, but one flesh.

9 What therefore God has joined together, let not man put asunder.

What do you learn about Jesus from these verses?

What do the references to God tell us about Him?

Who joins a man and his wife together into one flesh?

There are several conclusions in these verses:

in v. 5 Jesus states the reason why Moses wrote what he did. What is the reason?

in v. 6, 7 what is the cause for which a man leaves father and mother?

in v. 9 what is the "therefore" there for? Why is man not to put asunder or separate what God has joined together?

In the phrase, "one flesh", the greek word for flesh is *sarx*. It means body, human being. So one flesh means one body, one human being, as opposed to "twain" for which the greek word is *duo* meaning two.

God created man male and female so that in marriage, leaving each one's father and mother and cleaving to one another, the two would become one completed human being. The basis for this union is that God created man male and female.

God created man male and female so that in marriage, leaving father and mother, and cleaving to each other, they become one completed human being. The visible manifestation of this is seen in the children born from this relationship.

Now that we have studied what God's Word tells us, do you choose to believe that God created marriage to be between one man and one woman, and to be for as long as they live?

If you do, how should that impact your life?

 DAY 7

Begin your study with prayer. Ask the Lord to help you see and understand the invisible things of Him so that you will glorify Him as God.

> *"For the invisible things of Him from the creation of the world are clearly seen, being understood by the things that are made, even His eternal power and Godhead;" Romans 1: 20*

As you seek to know the Only True God by studying what He reveals about Himself through the pages of His Word, *the Bible*, you will read over and over that He is the Creator of the heavens and the earth and everything in them.

This knowledge requires a response: are you going to believe what God has revealed to you about Himself? If you do, are you going to honor and glorify Him in how you live the life He has given you?

In Romans 1: 17 we read

> *"For therein is the righteousness of God revealed from faith to faith: as it is written, The just shall live by faith."*

Let's look at what our response should be as we conclude this week's study.

Read the following passages three times; again one of those times being out loud. As you do, mark every reference to **God** with a blue triangle; don't forget the synonyms and pronouns, like *LORD*, **One**, **Lord.**

2 Kings 19: 15

And Hezekiah prayed before the LORD, and said, O LORD God of Israel, Which dwells between the cherubim, Thou art the God, even Thou alone, of all the kingdoms of the earth; Thou hast made heaven and earth.

Nehemiah 9: 6

Thou, even Thou, art LORD alone; Thou hast made heaven, the heaven of heavens, with all their host, the earth, and all things that are therein, the seas, and all that is therein, and Thou preservest them all; and the host of heaven worshippeth Thee.

Revelation 4: 2, 9-11

2 And immediately I was in the Spirit: and, behold, a throne was set in heaven, and One sat on the throne.

...

9 And when those beasts give glory and honor and thanks to Him that sat on the throne, Who liveth for ever and ever,

10 The four and twenty elders fall down before Him that sat on the throne, and worship Him that liveth for ever and ever, and cast their crowns before the throne, saying,

11 Thou art worthy, O Lord, to receive glory and honor and power: for Thou hast created all things, and for Thy pleasure they are and were created.

There is one more key word you should mark. It will help you notice more of what these passages are telling us. Have you noticed how *the throne* is repeated often? Under line each occurrence of *the throne*.

What does each reference to God, that you marked, tell you about God?

In each of these passages, we read the acknowledgement that God is the Creator of all, and we also see a response to that acknowledgement. List below the responses that you see in the verses. (Hint: in the first verse, the response is exactly what Hezekiah is doing. You might want to read 2 Kings 19: 8-19 to get a little more of what was going on in Hezekiah's life.)

According to the last verse you read in our passages, Rev. 4: 11, why are you alive?

Do you believe that God is the Creator of all? Why or why not?

Is God worthy to receive glory and honor and power? Why?

How can you glorify Him in your day-today life?
In how you spend your time? Your money?

In how you dress, talk, act?

In how you handle what happens in your life, how you relate to others,?

In how you do your job?

In what you choose to watch, read, be a part of?

" For the eyes of the LORD run to and fro throughout the whole earth, to shew Himself strong in the behalf of them whose heart is perfect toward Him." 2 Chronicles 16: 9a

📅 WEEK 3

THE ONLY TRUE

God is Sovereign

Our search of God's Word to know the Only True God has led us to see that He is Eternal, and He is the Creator of all that exists. We saw that He is One God, yet has 3 persons: God the Father, God the Son and God the Spirit.

We saw in our last day of study, in Revelation, that He has a throne set in heaven. In this week's study we are going to see why He sits on a throne: He is the Sovereign ruler of the whole universe!

Discovering what that means is going to be one of the most stabilizing and reassuring foundations for our lives. Understanding God's Sovereignty will empower us and free us to live the life for which He created us. God's Sovereignty is an amazing and liberating truth!

📅 DAY 1

Begin your study asking God to renew your mind today so that you will see Him and know Him more.

Read the passage below three times, once aloud, and as you do, mark every reference to *the LORD* with a blue triangle. Include the pronouns.

Psalm 103: 19-22

19 The LORD hath prepared His throne in the heavens; and His kingdom ruleth over all.
20 Bless the LORD, ye His angels, that excel in strength, that do His commandments, hearkening unto the voice of His Word.
21 Bless ye the LORD, all ye His hosts; ye ministers of His, that do His pleasure.
22 Bless the LORD, all His works in all places of His dominion: bless the LORD, O my soul.

The word used for God in this passage is LORD. It is typed with a first large capital letter and three small capital letters to distinguish the Hebrew word, Jehovah, from which it is translated. God reveals Himself to us in His Word through several names that tell us of His character, His attributes and His nature. The name, Jehovah, means *the unchanging, eternal, self-existent God.* It is the most frequently used name of God in the Old Testament.

List everything you learn about the LORD below. Go verse by verse and write exactly what the text tells you.

Specifically, what does verse 19 tell us about His kingdom?

There is another key word that is repeated several times in these verses: ***bless***. Mark that word in a different color of your choice.

Who is instructed to bless the LORD?

According to each marking of the word, *bless,* what can you notice about those who bless Him?

In this passage the word, *bless,* means *to worship God, to exalt and praise Him.*

How do the actions of those who bless God in these verses show His rule, His being Sovereign, and His being the Supreme Ruler over all?

📅 DAY 2

Begin this day with prayer.

The Bible is a Living Word: It explains Itself as we search out what It tells us. It is Its own best commentary. God uses many ways to show Himself to us, so He displays His Sovereignty throughout His Word in different instances. Therefore, when we study a matter, it is of utmost importance that we study the whole counsel of God on that matter throughout His Word. We must not build our understanding on an isolated verse or passage of Scripture, but on the whole of the Bible. In doing so diligently, we will see how the Bible interprets itself before our very eyes.

Today, we will continue our study of God's Sovereignty by looking at another key passage found in the book of Isaiah.

Read it three times through, and once aloud. Mark every reference to the Creator including pronouns and synonyms like ***Holy One*** with your blue triangle.

Isaiah 40: 12, 21-26

12 Who hath measured the waters in the hollow of His hand, and meted out heaven with the span, and comprehended the dust of the earth in a measure, and weighed the mountains in scales, and the hills in a balance?

...

21 Have ye not known? have ye not heard? hath it not been told you from the beginning? have ye not understood from the foundations of the earth?

22 It is He that sitteth upon the circle of the earth, and the inhabitants thereof are as grasshoppers; that stretcheth out the heavens as a curtain, and spreadeth them out as a tent to dwell in:

23 That bringeth the princes to nothing; He maketh the judges of the earth as vanity.

24 Yea, they shall not be planted; yea, they shall not be sown: yea, their stock shall not take root in the earth: and He shall also blow upon them, and they shall wither, and the whirlwind shall take them away as stubble.

25 To whom then will ye liken Me, or shall I be equal? saith the Holy One.

26 Lift up your eyes on high, and behold Who hath created these things, that bringeth out their host by number: He calleth them all by names by the greatness of His might, for that He is strong in power; not one faileth.

Did you notice the references to time as you read? Underline them with a yellow line.

The first verse you read, v. 12, was included in this passage because it gives the context needed for v. 21-26. What is the answer to the "Who" question that v. 12 asks?

In this passage we see several comparisons being made. Comparisons are important to notice and mark because they help us understand what God's Word is teaching us. Comparisons are noticeable when you see the words "*as*" or "*like*".

In verse 22 we see 3 comparisons. Mark them with a pencil by circling what is being compared to what, and connecting them. This simple marking tool helps you better observe what God is telling us.

Here is the first one:

> *inhabitants* ————— *grasshoppers*

1st comparison: the inhabitants of the earth are compared to grasshoppers.

2nd comparison:

3rd comparison:

Look at v. 26 again. At first, the word, "*things*", makes us wonder what this is talking about. In order to discern what it refers to, look at the beginning of the verse. Where are we told to lift our eyes to and look (behold)? Then, you see that God calls these "*things*" by names, and He numbers them. You also see that they do not fail... Now look up Psalm 147: 4 and let the Bible interpret itself to you. What are these *things*?

Look at the references to God that you marked with your blue triangle. Did you notice what is under His dominion or sovereignty? List what He controls and manages:

From what you have just studied is there anything or anyone equal to or greater than God?

What impact do these truths have for your life?

Can anything happen in your life that God is not in complete control of?

📅 DAY 3

Start your study with prayer, asking God to show you His glory.

Our study today is going to be in a chapter of the book of Daniel. Daniel was an Israelite who was taken captive along with his countrymen by the armies of the Babylonian empire. He was brought to Babylon and put in the service of the Babylonian king, Nebuchadnezzar. At that time, king Nebuchadnezzar was the most powerful ruler in the Middle East.

In Daniel 4, we read that king Nebuchadnezzar had a dream that scared him, and he asked Daniel to give him the meaning of that dream. This same scenario had happened before; you can read about the previous dream in chapter 2. Daniel had asked the Lord to show him what the dream was and what it meant, and God answered. In chapter 4 the king is quite troubled by this new dream and after asking all his wise men, and receiving no help at all, he calls Daniel. Once more the Lord gives Daniel the meaning of the dream: it is a warning from God to the king of what will happen to him if he does not *"break off thy sins by righteousness, and thine iniquities by shewing mercy to the poor"* (Daniel 4: 27).

The passage we will study today begins with king Nebuchadnezzar's response to God's warning.

Read it three times, once aloud, and mark every reference to God with a blue triangle, including the pronouns and synonyms like *the Most High*.

Daniel 4: 30-37

> **30** The king spake, and said, Is not this great Babylon, that I have built for the house of the kingdom by the might of my power, and for the honor of my majesty?
> **31** While the word was in the king's mouth, there fell a voice from heaven, saying, O king Nebuchadnezzar, to thee it is spoken; The kingdom is departed from thee.
> **32** And they shall drive thee from men, and thy dwelling shall be with the beasts of the field: they shall make thee to eat grass as oxen, and

seven times shall pass over thee, until thou know that the Most High ruleth in the kingdom of men, and giveth it to whomsoever He will.

33 The same hour was the thing fulfilled upon Nebuchadnezzar: and he was driven from men, and did eat grass as oxen, and his body was wet with the dew of heaven, till his hairs were grown like eagles' feathers, and his nails like birds' claws.

34 And at the end of days I Nebuchadnezzar lifted up mine eyes unto heaven, and mine understanding returned unto me, and I blessed the Most High, and I praised and honoured Him that liveth for ever, whose dominion is an everlasting dominion, and His kingdom is from generation to generation:

35 And all the inhabitants of the earth are reputed as nothing: and He doeth according to His will in the army of heaven, and among the inhabitants of the earth: and none can stay His hand, or say unto Him, What doest Thou?

36 At the same time my reason returned unto me; and for the glory of my kingdom, mine honor and brightness returned unto me; and I was established in my kingdom, and excellent majesty was added unto me.

37 Now I Nebuchadnezzar praise and extol and honor the King of heaven, all whose works are truth, and ways judgment: and those that walk in pride He is able to abase.

Now go back over these verses and mark every reference to Nebuchadnezzar with a purple **N**.

What happened to Nebuchadnezzar?

What did God want Nebuchadnezzar to recognize according to v. 32?

Did Nebuchadnezzar do this? What name does he use to refer to God in these verses?

What caused Nebuchadnezzar to acknowledge the Only True God's everlasting dominion?

What does this tell us about God and His power?

Look closely at v. 34-35 and list what Nebuchadnezzar says about God that he now recognizes. (watch for the details… the list is started for you)
v. 34 He lives for ever and ever
    His dominion is an everlasting dominion

In v. 35 Nebuchadnezzar says that God does according to His will in two places. What are they?

What does Nebuchadnezzar do now as a result of this experience in v. 37?

How does recognizing God as the Most High, Who rules over all, help us in our lives when difficulties come, things are unfair, hopeless, and we feel like we are facing more than we can bear?

What about when we are tempted to be angry with God or when we think we can do life our way?

📅 DAY 4

Ask God to help you with today's study.

There is a reassurance and a peace that comes from understanding that God is sovereign, that He rules over and controls all. When we realize and accept by faith that every circumstance of our lives can only happen if God first approves it, we feel secure.

Yet when difficulties and trials come, we are challenged.

We are forced to a greater level of faith, because we then have to accept that God's ways are not our ways. We have to reconcile ourselves with the fact that we are not always going to understand why He planned the trials and difficulties we experience.

Today, we need to look at verses that teach us about God's sovereignty over what we perceive as tragic. This is not easy to accept. Ask the Lord to give you the faith to take Him at His Word.

Ask Him help you live in the light of the truth of His Word.

Read the following passages three times, once aloud, and mark every reference to **God** including all the pronouns and synonyms with a blue triangle.

Deuteronomy 32: 39

See now that I, even I, am He, and there is no god with Me: I kill, and I make alive; I wound, and I heal: neither is there any that can deliver out of My hand.

1 Samuel 2: 6-10

6 The LORD killeth, and maketh alive: He bringeth down to the grave, and bringeth up.

7 The LORD maketh poor, and maketh rich: He bringeth low, and lifteth up.

8 He raiseth up the poor out of the dust, and lifteth up the beggar from the dunghill, to set them among princes, and to make them inherit the throne of glory: for the pillars of the earth are the LORD's, and He hath set the world upon them.

9 He will keep the feet of His saints, and the wicked shall be silent in darkness; for by strength shall no man prevail.

10 The adversaries of the LORD shall be broken to pieces; out of heaven shall He thunder upon them: the LORD shall judge the ends of the earth; and He shall give strength unto His king, and exalt the horn of His anointed.

Underline every reference to people in a color of your choice: all words that refer to people like *the poor*, *the beggar*, etc…

What do you learn about God in these verses?

What did you notice as you underlined every reference to the people?

List below everything that God is sovereign over according to these verses:

That will be enough for today. Continue to think about what you are seeing about the Only True God in His Word, remembering what Jesus said:

> *"And this is life eternal, that they might know Thee the Only True God, and Jesus Christ, Whom Thou hast sent." John 17: 3*

📅 DAY 5

Begin with prayer.

Today, we continue studying about God's sovereignty over what we see as undesirable. We need to ask God to increase our faith and our trust in Him as we grow in our knowledge of Him. The world in which we live values happiness, fairytale-like lives, and happy endings. Few understand the value of hardship, affliction and suffering. Opening our hearts to align ourselves with the eternal values of the Only True God is not natural for us to do. We need His help.

"Help Thou mine unbelief." Mark 9: 24b

Read the following three passages three times, once aloud, and mark every reference to **God** with a blue triangle including synonyms and pronouns. Then mark every reference to ***Jesus*** with a blue triangle with a cross in it.

Isaiah 45: 5-7

5 I am the LORD, and there is none else, there is no God beside me: I girded thee, though thou hast not known Me:
6 That they may know from the rising of the sun, and from the west, that there is none beside Me. I am the LORD, and there is none else.
7 I form the light, and create darkness: I make peace, and create evil: I the LORD do all these things.

John 19: 10-11

10 Then saith Pilate unto Him, Speakest Thou not unto me? knows Thou not that I have power to crucify Thee, and have power to release Thee?
11 Jesus answered, Thou couldest have no power at all against Me, except it were given thee from above: therefore he that delivered Me unto thee hath the greater sin.

1 Corinthians 10: 13

> There hath no temptation taken you but such as is common to man:
> but God is faithful, Who will not suffer you to be tempted above that
> ye are able; but will with the temptation also make a way to escape,
> that ye may be able to bear it.

Once again, write down everything you learn about God in these verses:

What do you learn about Jesus?

Look closely at what these verses tell us. List below what God controls
according to these verses:

1 Corinthians 10: 13 tells us that God is faithful. We are promised that we
will not be tempted with more than we can bear. 2 Peter 2: 9a says

"The Lord knoweth how to deliver the godly out of temptations"

Psalm 34: 19 says

*"Many are the afflictions of the righteous: but the L*ORD *delivers him out of them all."*

How can God promise what He does in 1 Corinthians 10: 13?

📅 DAY 6

Understanding the sovereignty of God has so many implications for us that it is important to take the time to think about this foundational truth.

Ask God to help you understand what His sovereignty means for your life.

Read the following passages three times, once aloud, and mark every reference to *God* with a blue triangle.

Isaiah 14: 24, 27

24 The LORD of hosts hath sworn, saying, Surely as I have thought, so shall it come to pass; and as I have purposed, so shall it stand:

...

27 For the LORD of hosts hath purposed, and who shall disannul it? and His hand is stretched out, and who shall turn It back?

Isaiah 46: 9-11

9 Remember the former things of old: for I am God, and there is none else; I am God, and there is none like me,

10 Declaring the end from the beginning, and from ancient times the things that are not yet done, saying, My counsel shall stand, and I will do all My pleasure:

11 Calling a ravenous bird from the east, the man that executeth My counsel from a far country: yea, I have spoken it, I will also bring it to pass; I have purposed it, I will also do it.

List below everything you learn from these verses about God.

You might have noticed as you read these verses three times that there are TWO words that are repeated in these verses that are key to what we learn about God. Go back to the verses and mark the words, ***purposed*** and ***counsel***, in a color of your choice. Either highlight, underline, circle, or draw a box around them.

The word, ***purposed***, in the Hebrew text of Isaiah 14 v. 24 & 27 is *ya'ats* which means to *deliberate* or *resolve.* In Isaiah 46 v. 11 it is *yatsar* which means to *mould*, as in what a potter does with clay, to *determine.*

The word, ***counsel***, in the Hebrew text of Isaiah 46 v. 10-11 is *etsah* which means *advice* or *plan.*

Reread the verses of Isaiah we are studying today, but this time read them with these meanings.

According to these verses, does God leave anything left up to "chance" or "fate"?

What do you learn about God's plan?

Can anyone or anything cancel God's plan?

In Isaiah 46 v.11 God gives two examples of how He plans. What are they?

Can you see that the Only True God has a plan, a purpose in everything He does? How does that apply to your life?

When we study God's Word to learn about Him and grow in our understanding and knowledge of Him, it is a very good practice to look up what we call cross-references. Those are other passages of God's Word that discuss the same topic and that can shed more light on what we are studying.

Romans 12 v. 2 tells us a little more about God's plan or will:

> *"And be not conformed to this world: but be ye transformed by the renewing of your mind, that ye may prove what is that good, and acceptable, and perfect, will of God."*

What does Romans 12 v. 2 tell us about God's will?

Now look at Romans 8: 28-29:

> *"And we know that all things work together for good to them that love God, to them who are the called according to His purpose. For whom He did foreknow, He also did predestinate to be conformed to the image of His Son, that He might be the first born among many brethren."*

Will you take God at His Word and believe that He has a plan for your life?

Are you ready to believe that because He is Sovereign, everything that happens in your life has been planned by Him to mould you and shape you into the image of His Son, the Lord Jesus Christ?

What difference does this make in your life to realize that God is Ruler over all, and that nothing can happen without His ultimate approval? Write out your thoughts.

📅 DAY 7

Understanding the sovereignty of God and what it means for our our lives is such an anchor for our souls. It is a milestone in our spiritual growth. It is a major part of the "firm foundation" we need on which to build our lives.

Yet, as we go about our daily lives, it is easy to forget. That is why starting each of our days sitting at the Lord's feet and hearing His Words, as Mary did in Luke 10: 39, is the very best habit we can form. The Lord Jesus said

> *"But one thing is needful: and Mary hath chosen that good part, which shall not be taken away from her." Luke 10:42*

In Romans 10: 17 we read

> *"So then faith cometh by hearing, and hearing by the Word of God."*

As we end our week of study about the sovereignty of God looking at a passage in Psalm 33, ask God to help you hear His Word and increase your faith. Ask Him to help you choose daily that good part that Mary chose, so that these foundational truths will not be taken away from you.

Read the following passage three times, once aloud, and mark every reference to *the LORD* with a blue triangle. Make sure to include all the pronouns that refer to Him.

Psalm 33: 6-15

6 By the word of the LORD were the heavens made; and all the host of them by the breath of His mouth.
7 He gathereth the waters of the sea together as an heap: He layeth up the depth in storehouses.
8 Let all the earth fear the LORD: let all the inhabitants of the world stand in awe of Him.
9 For He spake, and it was done; He commanded, and it stood fast.

> **10** The LORD bringeth the counsel of the heathen to nought: He maketh the devices of the people of none effect.
> **11** The counsel of the LORD standeth for ever, the thoughts of His heart to all generations.
> **12** Blessed is the nation whose God is the LORD; and the people whom He hath chosen for His own inheritance.
> **13** The LORD looketh from heaven; He beholdeth all the sons of men.
> **14** From the place of His habitation He looketh upon all the inhabitants of the earth.
> **15** He fashioneth their hearts alike; He considereth all their works.

Go back through the passage again and this time underline all the references to *people* with a color of your choice. Make sure you include ***inhabitants***, ***heathen***, ***nation*** and any other word that refers to people.

Now, look at your blue triangles and write down everything you learn from marking ***the LORD.***
Make sure you go verse by verse and observe carefully what each is telling us.

As an example of something not to miss, we learn in v.14 that the Lord has a habitation, a place where He lives.

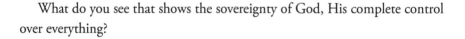

What do you see that shows the sovereignty of God, His complete control over everything?

What did you learn from underlining the references to people?

How do any of these truths apply to people today?

How do these truths apply to the circumstances you are going through right now?

There are so many more passages of God's Word that affirm over and over again that the Only True God reveals Himself to us as being the Supreme Ruler over all the universe and everything in it. He has a purpose, a counsel, and it will be accomplished. Nothing He created can prevent that, and nothing can happen that He is not in complete control of.

Realizing this causes us to stand in awe of Him!

It brings us to realize that we obviously don't understand all about His ways or His thoughts. We begin to see that the way we think is much more limited and finite than the way He thinks. Yet, we know we can trust this One Who is eternal, Who created us and gives us the breath of life moment by moment, and Who controls everything that happens.

"For I know the thoughts that I think towards you, saith the the LORD, thoughts of peace, and not of evil, to give you an expected end." Jeremiah 29: 11

What a peace and quiet confidence we can gain from understanding and accepting what God says about Himself in His Word. Close your study today by telling God what fills your heart as a result of what you have learned these past three weeks.

 **WEEK 4**

THE ONLY TRUE

God is Omniscient, Omnipresent and Omnipotent

If you decided to read through the Bible from cover to cover to know Who God is, and if you kept a notebook in which you noted everything you learn about Him, it would completely change your life and the way you see things. It wouldn't take long until you discovered that He knows everything; He is everywhere and He can do anything He wants to.

In this week's study we are going to look at the following three attributes of God: His omniscience, His omnipresence and His omnipotence..

Omni means all.

Science means knowledge. God is omniscient because He knows all.

God is omnipresent because He is present everywhere.

Potent means powerful. God is omnipotent because He is all powerful.

DAY 1

Begin with prayer.

Read the following passage three times, once aloud, and mark every reference to **LORD** with a blue triangle. Don't forget the pronouns.

Psalm 139: 1-6

1 O LORD, Thou hast searched me, and known me.

2 Thou knowest my downsitting and mine uprising, Thou understandest my thought afar off.

3 Thou compassest my path and my lying down, and art acquainted with all my ways.

4 For there is not a word in my tongue, but, lo, O LORD, Thou knowest it altogether.

5 Thou hast beset me behind and before, and laid Thine hand upon me.

6 Such knowledge is too wonderful for me; it is high, I cannot attain unto it.

What do you learn about God in these verses? What is He able to do? What does that tell you about Him?

Go through the passage again and this time draw an orange circle around every reference to the writer. They are the pronouns *me, I, my, mine*.

Next, underline ***known, knowest*** and ***knowledge***, in a different color of your choice.

List below everything that God knows according to these verses:

As we go through our week of studying about God's omniscience, His omnipresence, and His omnipotence it will be valuable to put our observations into a chart. Fill the chart below with each verse reference and a summary of how the verse shows each attribute, as you go through all the passages we will study this week. The chart is started to help you see how to do this.

Omniscient	Omnipresent	Omnipotent
Psalm 139 v. 1 God knows me *v. 2 He knows when I sit down* *and when I get up* *v. 2 He understands my thoughts*		

 # DAY 2

"O God, Thou art my God; early will I seek Thee" Psalm 63: 1a

Seek the Lord in prayer as you begin today's study.

Psalm 139 was written by David under the inspiration of the Holy Spirit, and studying it gives us much insight about God. So today we continue with the next section of Psalm 139. Today as we continue studying Psalm 139, make sure you fill out the chart we started yesterday.

Read the following passage three times, once aloud, marking every reference to **God** with a blue triangle including pronouns.

Psalm 139: 7-12

7 Whither shall I go from Thy Spirit? or whither shall I flee from Thy presence?
8 If I ascend up into heaven, Thou art there: if I make my bed in hell, behold, Thou art there.
9 If I take the wings of the morning, and dwell in the uttermost parts of the sea;
10 Even there shall Thy hand lead me, and Thy right hand shall hold me.
11 If I say, Surely the darkness shall cover me; even the night shall be light about me.
12 Yea, the darkness hideth not from Thee; but the night shineth as the day: the darkness and the light are both alike to Thee.

Go through these verses again and this time circle each pronoun: *I, my, me*.
Did you notice any evidence of the "omnis" of God in this passage? Which ones?

Make sure to put them in the chart.

As you circled the pronouns *I, me* and *my*, did you think this also applies to you? Write down why.

List all the places or locations that are mentioned in these verses about where God is:

Is there any place or location where you can be that God isn't there with you?

According to these verses, can anything be hidden from God?

What does God do for you, wherever you are?

Thinking about the verses we have looked at so far in Psalm 139, how does it make you feel to realize that God knows you in all these ways?

Conclude your study today with talking to the Lord about how you feel about what you have studied.

📅 DAY 3

Today, we will continue looking at amazing truths we read in Psalm 139 about the Only True God. We have already studied two of those verses in our previous chapter about God, our Creator, but today we will study these for more truths we can learn about God's character and attributes.

Ask the Lord to open the eyes of your understanding so that you might increase in your knowledge of Him, and so that you might love Him more as a result.

Read the verses below three times, once aloud, and mark every reference to **God**, including the pronouns with a blue triangle. Also, continue to circle each **I, me**, and **my**.

Psalm 139: 13-18, 23-24

13 For Thou hast possessed my reins: Thou hast covered me in my mother's womb.
14 I will praise Thee; for I am fearfully and wonderfully made: marvelous are Thy works; and that my soul knoweth right well.
15 My substance was not hid from Thee, when I was made in secret, and curiously wrought in the lowest parts of the earth.
16 Thine eyes did see my substance, yet being unperfect; and in Thy book all my members were written, which in continuance were fashioned, when as yet there was none of them.
17 How precious also are Thy thoughts unto me, O God! how great is the sum of them!
18 If I should count them, they are more in number than the sand: when I awake, I am still with Thee.

...

23 Search me, O God, and know my heart: try me, and know my thoughts:
24 And see if there be any wicked way in me, and lead me in the way everlasting.

These verses are so full of awe-inspiring truths about God.

If you think about what this is saying, and look carefully, you will notice that there are two areas or locations being especially noted. They are described as places that God sees and knows. They are places no one else can see.

In what hidden locations does God see what concerns us individually? *(hint: one is in v.13, and it is referred to again in v. 15, and the second one is in v. 23)*

What exactly does God see according to these verses?

According to v. 16 where were *all my members* written?

When were *all my members* written? And when did God see *my substance*?

Looking at all the personal pronouns you circled, *I*, *me* and *my,* and looking at the verbs that they are connected to, we can make a list of what God does for us. Continue the list that is started for you below.

What God does for me:

v. 13 He possesses my reins (reins literally means kidneys, and figuratively it means mind)

v. 13 He covered me while I was in my mother's womb

Is there anything that God doesn't know about you?

What does that tell us about our Only True God?

Write about what that means for your day-to-day life.

Carefully read the following passages and verses.

Write out what you learn about God's presence and about His knowledge.

Think about how it applies to your life, and write down what the Lord impresses upon your heart.

Genesis 16: 13

(Read the whole chapter to see how Hagar came to know God this way)
And she called the name of the LORD that spake unto her, Thou God seest me: for she said, Have I also here looked after Him that seeth me?

Joshua 1: 9

Have I not commanded thee ? Be strong and of a good courage; be not afraid, neither be thou dismayed: for the LORD Thy God is with thee whithersoever thou goest.

Job 23: 10

But He knoweth the way that I take: when He hath tried me, I shall come forth as gold.

Psalm 94: 7-11

7 Yet they say, The LORD shall not see, neither shall the God of Jacob regard it.

8 Understand, ye brutish among the people: and ye fools, when will ye be wise?

9 He that planted the ear, shall He nor hear? He that formed the eye, shall He not see?

10 He that chastiseth the heathen, shall He not correct? He that teacheth man knowledge, shall He not know?

11 The LORD knoweth the thoughts of man, that they are vanity.

Jeremiah 23: 23-24

23 Am I a God at hand, saith the LORD, and not a God afar off?

24 Can any hide himself in secret places that I shall not see him? saith the LORD. Do not I fill heaven and earth? saith the LORD?

Matthew 6: 25-34

25 Therefore say I unto you, Take no thought for your life, what ye shall eat, or what ye shall drink; nor yet for your body, what ye shall put on. Is not the life more than meat, and the body more than raiment?

26 Behold the fowls of the air: for they sow not, neither do they reap, nor gather into barns; yet your heavenly Father feedeth them. Are ye not much better than they?

27 Which of you by taking thought can add one cubit unto his stature?

28 And why take ye thought for raiment? Consider the lilies of the field, how they grow; they toil not, neither do they spin:

29 And yet I say unto you, That even Solomon in all his glory was not arrayed like one of these.

30 Wherefore if God so clothe the grass of the field, which today is, and to morrow is cast into the oven, shall He not much more clothe you, O ye of little faith?

31 Therefore take no thought, saying, What shall we eat? or, What shall we drink? or, Wherewithal shall we be clothed?

32 (For after all these things do the Gentiles seek:) for your heavenly Father knoweth that ye have need of all these things.

33 But seek ye first the kingdom of God, and His righteousness; and all these things shall be added unto you.

34 Take therefore no thought for the morrow: for the morrow shall take thought for the things of itself. Sufficient unto the day is the evil thereof.

Matthew 28: 19-20

19 Go ye therefore, and teach all nations, baptizing them in the name of the Father, and of the Son, and of the Holy Ghost:

20 Teaching them to observe all things whatsoever I have commanded you: and, lo, I am with you alway, even unto the end of the world. Amen.

Hebrews 13: 5-6

5 Let your conversation be without covetousness; and be content with such things as ye have: for He hath said , I will never leave thee, nor forsake thee.

6 So that we may boldly say, The Lord is my helper, and I will not fear what man may do unto me.

DAY 4

We are halfway through this study!

You are to be commended for being faithful and committed. Sometimes, we can get weary in a study like this one. Our desire to know God is not as strong as it was when we first started. It's ok. He knows and understands us better than we understand ourselves.

> *"For He knoweth our frame; He remembereth that we are dust."*
> *Psalm 103: 14*

This is a good time to take a little longer to pray and ask the Lord for His help to keep calm and study on!

> *"Therefore, my beloved brethren, be ye stedfast, unmoveable, always abounding in the work of the Lord, forasmuch as ye know that your labor is not in vain in the Lord." 1 Corinthians 15: 58*

Today, we will look at several small portions of Scriptures. As you go through them, remember to add your observations to the chart we started on day 1 of this week: God's Omniscience, His Omnipresence, and His Omnipotence.

Read the following verses three times, once aloud. Mark every reference to *God* and the *LORD* with a blue triangle.

2 Chronicles 16: 7-9

7 And at that time Hanani the seer came to Asa king of Judah, and said unto him, Because thou hast relied on the king of Syria, and not relied on the LORD thy God, therefore is the host of the king of Syria escaped out of thine hand.

8 Were not the Ethiopians and the Lubims a huge host, with very many chariots and horsemen? yet, because thou didst rely on the LORD, He delivered them into thine hand.

9 For the eyes of the LORD run to and fro throughout the whole earth, to shew Himself strong in the behalf of them whose heart is perfect toward Him. Herein thou hast done foolishly: therefore from henceforth thou shalt have wars.

Psalm 44: 20-21

20 If we have forgotten the Name of our God, or stretched out our hands to a strange god;
21 Shall not God search this out? for He knoweth the secrets of the heart.

Proverbs 15: 3

The eyes of the LORD are in every place , beholding
the evil and the good.

Jeremiah 12: 3a

But Thou, O LORD, knowest me: Thou hast seen me, and tried mine heart toward Thee.

Now, go back over the verses and mark every reference to *the heart* with a red heart.

What do you learn from each passage about God's omniscience and our hearts?

What else do you learn from marking the references to the Lord in these verses? Look carefully, verse by verse. Do you see any of His other attributes, besides His omniscience?

What did marking the references to the heart show you?

What does king Asa's reliance on the king of Syria tell us about his heart?

Does the truth of 2 Chronicles 16:9a apply to us? Explain your answer.

 # DAY 5

Ask the Lord for His help today as you continue in this study.

A few more passages of Scripture show us just how total and infinite God's knowledge is.

Read the following verses three times, once aloud and mark every reference to **God** with a blue triangle, and every reference to **Jesus** with a cross inside a blue triangle. Include any synonyms and pronouns.

Also, continue marking every reference to **the heart** with a red heart shape over the word.

Matthew 10: 29-31

29 Are not two sparrows sold for a farthing? and one of them shall not fall on the ground without your Father.

30 But the very hairs of your head are all numbered.

31 Fear ye not therefore, ye are of more value than many sparrows.

Luke 16: 14-15

14 And the Pharisees also, who were covetous, heard all these things: and they derided Him.

15 And He said unto them, Ye are they which justify yourselves before men: but God knoweth your hearts: for that which is highly esteemed among men is abomination in the sight of God.

Hebrews 4: 13

Neither is there any creature that is not manifest in His sight: but all things are naked and opened unto the eyes of Him with Whom we have to do.

What do you learn from each passage about God's omniscience and the heart of man?

According to what you have read, is there anything that God doesn't know?

Look at this verse and think about God's omnipresence.

Deuteronomy 31: 8

And the LORD, He it is that doth go before thee; He will be with thee, He will not fail thee, neither forsake thee: fear not, neither be dismayed.

Is there any time or place where the Lord is not with you?

It is difficult for us to understand how God can be with everyone, everywhere, all the time, because our minds are not infinite like His is. Our understanding is limited. So truths like what we have just read have to be accepted by faith.

Do you believe what you have read today?

If so, write below what this means for your day-to-day life, for your moment-by-moment choices and decisions:

 # DAY 6

Begin your time of study with prayer.

Today, we are going to study a passage that teaches us about God's amazing and total power to do whatever He wants, His omnipotence.

Judah's king Jehoshaphat was faced with an impossible situation when several great armies were coming against him. He chose to call upon God. Read the portion of his prayer below three times, once aloud, and mark every reference to God with a blue triangle including the pronouns and synonyms.

2 Chronicles 20: 5-12

5 And Jehoshaphat stood in the congregation of Judah and Jerusalem, in the house of the LORD, before the new court,

6 And said, O LORD God of our fathers, art Thou not God in heaven? and rulest not Thou over all the kingdoms of the heathen? and in Thine hand is there not power and might, so that none is able to withstand Thee?

7 Art not Thou our God, Who didst drive out the inhabitants of this land before Thy people Israel, and gavest it to the seed of Abraham Thy friend for ever?

8 And they dwelt therein, and have built Thee a sanctuary therein for Thy Name, saying,

9 If, when evil cometh upon us, as the sword, judgment, or pestilence, or famine, we stand before this house, and in Thy presence, (for Thy Name is in this house,) and cry unto Thee in our affliction, then Thou wilt hear and help.

10 And now, behold, the children of Ammon and Moab and mount Seir, whom Thou wouldest not let Israel invade, when they came out of the land of Egypt, but they turned from them, and destroyed them not:

11 Behold, I say, how they reward us, to come to cast us out of Thy possession, which Thou hast given us to inherit.

12 O our God, wilt Thou not judge them? for we have no might against this great company that cometh against us; neither know we what to do: but our eyes are upon Thee.

What a prayer! It gives a very real glimpse into the heart of this king, Jehoshaphat. It establishes the certainty of Who God is.

Make a list below of what Jehoshaphat remembers that the Lord has done for His people Israel so far:

How does remembering what the Lord has done in the past help Jehoshaphat in this situation?

It would be well worth your time to read the rest of 2 Chronicles 20 and see how the Lord responds to Jehoshaphat's prayer.

Do you see a lesson for your life in how this account shows God's omnipotence?

Is there a pattern you can follow when you don't know what to do?

Don't forget to add what you learn to the chart we started on day 1.

 **DAY 7**

Begin your study today by thinking about all that we have seen this week about God.

Reflect upon the truths that He is present everywhere, He knows everything, and He is all powerful.

Talk with Him about what you have learned so far, and ask Him to help you with today's study.

Today, we will study four more passages that show us the infinite power of our Only True God.

Read them three times, once aloud, and mark every reference to God with a blue triangle including pronouns.

Genesis 18: 10-14

10 And He said, I will certainly return unto thee according to the time of life; and, lo, Sarah thy wife shall have a son. And Sarah heard it in the tent door, which was behind Him.

11 Now Abraham and Sarah were old and well stricken in age; and it ceased to be with Sarah after the manner of women.

12 Therefore Sarah laughed within herself, saying, After I am waxed old shall I have pleasure, my lord being old also?

13 And the LORD said unto Abraham, Wherefore did Sarah laugh, saying, Shall I of a surety bear a child which am old?

14 Is any thing too hard for the LORD? At the time appointed I will return unto thee, according to the time of life, and Sarah will have a son.

Jeremiah 32: 17-19, 26-27

17 Ah Lord God! behold, Thou hast made the heavens and the earth by Thy great power and stretched out arm, and there is nothing too hard for Thee:

18 Thou showest lovingkindness unto thousands, and recompensest the iniquity of the fathers unto the bosom of their children after them: the Great, the Mighty God, the LORD of Hosts, is His name,

19 Great in counsel, and mighty in work: for Thine eyes are open upon all the ways of the sons of men: to give every one according to his ways, and according to the fruit of his doings:

…

26 Then came the word of the LORD unto Jeremiah, saying,

27 Behold, I am the LORD, the God of all flesh: is there any thing too hard for me?

Daniel 2: 20-22

20 Daniel answered and said, Blessed be the name of God for ever and ever: for wisdom and might are His:

21 And He changeth the times and the seasons: He removeth kings, and setteth up kings: He giveth wisdom unto the wise, and knowledge to them that know understanding:

22 He revealed the deep and secret things: He knoweth what is in the darkness, and the light dwelleth with Him.

Luke 1: 36-37

36 And, behold, thy cousin Elisabeth, she hath also conceived a son in her old age: and this is the sixth month with her, who was called barren.

37 For with God nothing shall be impossible.

What do you learn about God from marking every reference to Him in these passages? List what each marking tells you.

What specific attributes of God are described in these passages?

Write down what we see God do in these verses that man cannot do:

These are only a few of the multiple examples of God's infinite power that His Word shows us. We could do a study on the power of God throughout Scripture, listing everything He does that is impossible to man, and it would impact us for life!

How can knowing the truth of God's infinite power help you personally with whatever is happening in your life today?

Complete the chart we started on Day 1 this week with what we studied today.

Isn't it reassuring and comforting to know that even if we don't understand how things will work out, or why things are happening the way they are, God knows all about it?

He is well aware of all of our circumstances, and He will never leave us!

There is only one thing that can never be taken away from us in this life and that is our Only True God!

Knowing that He can do anything He wants to can give us the greatest sense of security.

What peace and rest there is in living our daily lives in that constant reality!

📅 WEEK 5

THE ONLY TRUE

God is Righteousness, Justice and Truth

Are you in awe of the Only True God that we are getting to know as we study His Word?

He is so infinite, so far beyond what our limited minds can understand or imagine!

Yet, He created us in His image! Isn't that completely amazing?

To recap what we have learned and verified from God's own Word to us so far, we understand that the Only True God is eternal: He has always been and will always be. We saw that He created everything that exists and that He is in complete control of all.

Our study, then, took us to where God reveals Himself to us as omniscient, the One who knows all; omnipotent, the One who can do anything and everything; and omnipresent, the One who is always present everywhere.

Whith such infinite attributes, should we be afraid of what He might do to us? Especially, since He knows everything about us...

How do we know that He is going to use all His power and sovereignty in such a way that we can fully relate to Him and trust Him?

This week we are going to see three key attributes of the Only True God that will give us courage to trust and obey Him no matter what happens in our lives. If we get to know His righteousness, His justice, and His truth, we will gain an inner peace that will make us want to live according to everything His Word teaches us.

 # DAY 1

Begin with prayer.

Read the passage for today three times, once aloud, and mark every reference to **God** with a blue triangle, including all the pronouns. Also, mark the word, *truth,* with a green T.

Psalm 89: 5-14

5 And the heavens shall praise thy wonders, O Lord: thy faithfulness also in the congregation of the saints.

6 For who in the heaven can be compared unto the Lord? who among the sons of the mighty can be likened unto the Lord?

7 God is greatly to be feared in the assembly of the saints, and to be had in reverence of all them that are about Him.

8 O Lord God of hosts, who is a strong Lord like unto Thee? or to thy faithfulness round about Thee?

9 Thou rulest the raging of the sea: when the waves thereof arise, Thou stillest them.

10 Thou hast broken Rahab in pieces, as one that is slain; Thou hast scattered Thine enemies with Thy strong arm.

11 The heavens are Thine, the earth also is Thine: as for the world and the fulness thereof, Thou hast founded them.

12 The north and the south Thou hast created them: Tabor and Herman shall rejoice in Thy name.

13 Thou hast a mighty arm: strong is Thy hand, and high is Thy right hand.

14 Justice and judgment are the habitation of Thy throne: mercy and truth shall go before Thy face.

What did you learn about God from marking these verses?

What gives God His authority? Look at v.11.

What two things make up the habitation of His throne? Habitation is used in the sense of establishment, so these are the basis upon which God's throne is established.

What goes before His face? In other words, what characterizes His rule?

We need to understand the meaning of the words we read in God's Word.

The Hebrew word for justice is *tsedeq*, which means *equity, just, right.*
Equity includes a sense of equality in evaluation, which implies right evaluation. Fairness would be another way that we refer to justice in our lives.

The Hebrew word for truth is *emeth*, which means *stability, certainty, truth, trustworthiness.*
Certainty implies accuracy and exactitude, so that includes unchanging and unalterable. It is significant that the meaning of the Hebrew word includes trustworthiness; it shows us that important connection between truth and trust.
My Pastor defines truth as something that can be defined as true for all people, in all places, all the time.

How does this description of Who God is apply to your life? What does it mean in relationship to what God has planned for your life?

Can you trust God? Why?

 DAY 2

Seek the Lord in prayer: ask Him to show you what He wants you to learn and understand about Him today. Specifically, ask Him to show you what it means that He is Justice.

How does God reveal Himself to us in the passages of His Word printed out below?

Read them three times, once aloud, and mark every reference to Him with a blue triangle, including all the pronouns.

Deuteronomy 10: 17-18

17 For the LORD your God is God of gods, and Lord of lords, a great God, a mighty, and a terrible, which regardeth not persons, nor taketh reward:

18 He doth execute the judgment of the fatherless and widow, and loveth the stranger, in giving him food and raiment.

Deuteronomy 32: 3-4

3 Because I will publish the name of the LORD: ascribe ye greatness unto our God.

4 He is the Rock, His work is perfect: for all His ways are judgment: a God of truth and without iniquity, just and right is He.

Psalm 111: 7

The works of His hands are verity and judgment; all His commandments are sure.

How is God described in these verses?

Did you notice a word that appears in all four of these passages describing God and the way He works?

Judgment is in all of these passages. Mark it with a red capital *J* over it. Also, mark the word *just* in the same way when you see it.

The Hebrew word used for judgment in all these passages is the same word: *mishpat*. It means *justice, "rightness rooted in God's character"*, according to the Theological Wordbook of the Old Testament. [1]

The Hebrew word for just is t*saddiyq*, which means *just, lawful, or righteous.* It suggests conformity to an ethical or moral standard, decisions made according to the truth and without partiality.

The concept of justice is actually very important to all of us. How many times have you heard someone say, "that's not fair!"? Think about that. What is fairness? What is justice? Why is that so important to us?

We are upset when we see injustice or when we hear of matters that have not been handled with equality for all the parties involved.

The typical symbol for the judicial branch of government and for law practices is a scale with equal weights on both sides. That represents the basic human need for, and right to justice.

The definition of the Hebrew words for judgment and just give us some understanding of what justice is: we see that it includes truth and righteousness. Yet, it still seems difficult to fully understand what justice is.

This is when learning how to do a word study in God's Word becomes a valuable tool. We can take the Hebrew words that we see used in our passages,

1| R.Laird Harris, Gleason L. Archer, Jr., Bruce K. Waltke, Theological Workbook of the Old Testament, (Chicago, Moody Publishers, 1980) 948 and using a concordance such as Strong's Exhaustive Concordance, we can look up other verses in which the same word is used. In doing so, we will see how that word is used, in what context, and in relationship to what subject. Those observations will help us get a deeper understanding of the word we are studying and what it means.

In this case we will see what is described as just.

The words we will study are:

Judgment:
> Strong's # 4941: *mishpat*
> Meaning: verdict, sentence, law, justice, right, privilege, style

Just:
> Strong's # 6662: *tsaddiyq*
> Meaning: just, lawful, righteous

Beginning with the verses that we read today, and continuing with the additional verses, write out what you learn about justice, about being just. With what is it connected? Who does it impact? Is it a good impact or a negative one? Be diligent. These are a lot of verses. Write out what the Lord shows you.

Deuteronomy 10: 17-18

> **17** For the LORD your God is God of gods, and Lord of lords, a great God, a mighty, and a terrible, which regardeth not persons, nor taketh reward:
> **18** He doth execute the judgment of the fatherless and widow, and loveth the stranger, in giving him food and raiment.

Deuteronomy 32: 3-4

3 Because I will publish the name of the LORD: ascribe ye greatness unto our God.

4 He is the Rock, His work is perfect: for all His ways are judgment: a God of truth and without iniquity, just and right is He.

Psalm 111: 7

The works of His hands are verity and judgment; all His commandments are sure.

Leviticus 19: 15 *(respect in this verse means lift)*

Ye shall do no unrighteousness in judgment: thou shalt not respect the person of the poor, nor honour the person of the mighty: but in righteousness shalt you judge thy neighbor.

Leviticus 19: 35-36

35 Ye shall do no unrighteousness in judgment, in mete yard, in weight, or in measure.

36 Just balances, just weights, a just ephah, and a just hin, shall ye have: I am the LORD your God, which brought you out of the land of Egypt.

Deuteronomy 1: 17a *(respect in this verse means scrutinize, recognize, acknowledge)*

Ye shall not respect persons in judgment: but ye shall hear the small as well as the great; ye shall not be afraid of the face of man; for the judgment is God's:

Deuteronomy 16: 18-19 *(wrest means stretch, bend)*

18 Judges and officers shalt thou make thee in all thy gates, which the LORD thy God giveth thee, throughout thy tribes: and they shall judge the people with just judgment.
19 Thou shalt not wrest judgment; thou shalt not respect persons, neither take a gift: for a gift doth blind the eyes of the wise, and pervert the words of the righteous.

Deuteronomy 24: 17

Thou shalt not pervert the judgment of the stranger, nor of the fatherless; nor take a widow's raiment to pledge:

Ecclesiastes 7: 20

For there is not a just man upon earth, that doeth good, and sinneth not.

Isaiah 26: 7

The way of the just is uprightness: thou, most upright, doth weigh the path of the just.

Isaiah 59: 14-15 *(these verses describe absence of justice)*

14 And judgment is turned away backward, and justice standeth afar off: for truth is fallen in the street, and equity cannot enter.
15 Yea, truth faileth: and he that departeth from evil taketh himself a prey: and the LORD saw it, and it displeased Him that there was no judgment.

Jeremiah 22: 3

Thus saith the LORD; Execute ye judgment and righteousness, and deliver the spoiled out of the hand of the oppressor: and do no wrong, do no violence to the stranger, the fatherless, nor the widow, neither shed innocent blood in this place.

Ezekiel 18: 5

But if a man be just, and do that which is lawful and right,

Zephaniah 3: 5

The just LORD is in the midst thereof: He will do no iniquity: every morning doth He bring His judgment to light, He faileth not; but the unjust knoweth no shame.

Zechariah 8: 16

These are the things that ye shall do; Speak ye every man the truth to his neighbor; execute the judgment of truth and peace in your gates:

Conclude your study today by asking the Lord to give you a summary of what justice is, and write it down.

Now think about what it means in your life to know that God is Justice. How does that affect you?

📅 DAY 3

Looking at a few more verses about the Only True God, today will be a lighter day.

Begin with prayer.

Read the following verses three times, as usual, and once aloud. Reading out loud helps you think about what you are reading. Mark the references to **God** with a blue triangle and the words ***Judge, judgment, justly*** with a red ***J***.

Isaiah 30: 18

And therefore will the LORD wait, that He may be gracious unto you, and therefore will He be exalted, that He may have mercy upon you: for the LORD is a God of judgment: blessed are all they that wait for Him.

Genesis 18: 25

That be far from Thee to do after this manner, to slay the righteous with the wicked: and that the righteous should be as the wicked, that be far from Thee: Shall not the Judge of all the earth do right?

Micah 6: 8

He hath shewed thee, O man, what is good; and what doth the LORD require of thee, but to do justly, and to love mercy, and to walk humbly with thy God?

List everything you learn about God from marking the references to Him.

As you look at your markings of Judge, judgment and justly, what do you learn from these?

How is the justice of God revealed in these verses?

We have already seen that God created us in His image. As you now learn about God's justice, what do you think He wants to see in us, in relationship to justice?

Take a moment now to reflect on all that we have seen about justice from the Word of God.

As you do, think about all the times you have heard that God isn't fair, or the times you hear people question God's justice. There definitely are times and situations in which we might be tempted to question the fairness and justice of God. How will you handle those times now that you have studied how God reveals Himself to you in His Word?

Do all the verses we have studied in these last two days have an effect on your desire to trust in the Only True God?

 **DAY 4**

We all love happy endings.

Growing up, we learn about all the classic fairy tales, and we dream of a fairytale-like life.

There is nothing wrong with that... except that it sets us up with high expectations, and when difficulties and trials come, we don't understand. We question God, and we can become bitter and resentful.

We have studied that God is all powerful, that He knows everything, and that He is everywhere. With that kind of power and ability, we can be led to think that He can give us a fairytale-like life.

However, when suffering comes into our lives, and we are struggling with pain, we can be tempted to think that God is doing us wrong.

Can God do wrong? Can He be unrighteous?

Ask God to help you see the truth about Him that will set you free from believing the lies that our enemy, the devil, wants to use to deceive us.

Read the next set of verses three times, once aloud, and mark every reference to **God** with a blue triangle.

Psalm 71: 18-20

18 Now also when I am old and gray headed, O God, forsake me not; until I have shewed Thy strength unto this generation, and Thy power to everyone that is to come.
19 Thy righteousness also, O God, is very high, Who hast done great things: O God, who is like unto Thee!
20 Thou, Which hast shewed me great and sore troubles, shalt quicken me again, and shalt bring me up again from the depths of the earth.

Psalm 119: 142

Thy righteousness is an everlasting righteousness, and Thy law is the truth.

Psalm 145: 17-20

17 The LORD is righteous in all His ways, and holy in all His works.
18 The LORD is nigh unto all them that call upon Him, to all that call upon Him in truth.
19 He will fulfill the desires of them that fear Him: He also will hear their cry, and will save them.
20 The LORD preserveth all them that love Him: but all the wicked will He destroy.

Romans 9: 14

What shall we say then? Is there unrighteousness with God? God forbid.

Mark *righteousness* and *righteous* with an **R** in a color of your choice. Then, mark *unrighteousness* with that same **R**, but put a slash though it.

Mark *truth* with a **T** as you did before.

Draw a wavy line under any reference to difficult situations, such as *troubles, cry*, etc...

Write out everything you learned from marking the references to God.

Now list what you learned about righteousness, righteous.

What does God's righteousness provide for those who fear and love Him, according to Psalm 145: 19, 20? To fear in this context means to respect, honor, or stand in awe of.

Think about difficult situations, struggles, even death. Do these events in our lives mean that God is not righteous? Write the reasons for your answer.

Did you see the reference to time in Psalm 119: 142? What does that tell us about the righteousness of God?

Is there any benefit to knowing these truths about God's righteousness?

 DAY 5

In the book of Revelation, which is the last book in God's Word, *the Bible*, we are given a preview of events that are yet to come.

In His infinite wisdom God gives us this sneak peak so that we can understand more about His total Righteousness, Justice and Truth.

Ask Him to open the eyes of your understanding as you study His Word today, so that you can find the knowledge of the Only True God.

Read the following passages three times, once aloud. Mark every reference to **God** with a blue triangle including pronouns and synonyms.

Revelation 15: 1-4

1 And I saw another sign in heaven, great and marvelous, seven angels having the seven last plagues; for in them is filled up the wrath of God.
2 And I saw as it were a sea of glass mingled with fire: and them that had gotten the victory over the beast, and over his image, and over his mark, and over the number of his name, stand on the sea of glass, having the harps of God.
3 And they sing the song of Moses the servant of God, and the song of the Lamb, saying, Great and marvelous are Thy works, Lord God Almighty; just and true are Thy ways, Thou King of saints.
4 Who shall not fear Thee, O Lord, and glorify Thy name? for Thou only art holy: for all nations shall come and worship before Thee; for Thy judgments are made manifest.

Revelation 16: 4-7

4 And the third angel poured out his vial upon the rivers and fountains of waters; and they became blood.
5 And I heard the angel of the waters say, Thou art righteous, O Lord, which art, and wast, and shalt be, because Thou hast judged thus.

6 For they have shed the blood of saints and prophets, and Thou hast given them blood to drink; for they are worthy.

7 And I heard another out of the altar say, Even so, Lord God Almighty, true and righteous are Thy judgments.

Mark every word *righteous* with an *R* as you did before.

Mark every occurrence of the words *truth* and *true* with a *T* as you did before.

Mark every reference to *just, judged* and *judgments* with a *J* as you did before.

Finally, mark the references to God's judgments such as *plagues, wrath* and *blood* with a red lightning bolt like this:

List everything you learn about God from these verses:

How is God's justice manifested in these verses?

Remember how the word, "for", is usually a term of conclusion in God's Word?

There are three "for"s in Rev. 15:4, and two in Rev 16:6. Can you see the conclusions that are being made?

Ask the Lord to show you what these conclusions are.

The first one is "for Thou only art holy". For what reason is this "for" there? The answer is in verse 3: because God's ways are just and true.

Why will all nations come and worship before Him? The next "for" answers that question. Write it out:

129

What is the relationship between God's righteousness and His justice according to what you read in these verses?

Is this what people understand about God? What do people say about God's righteousness and justice?

From what you have seen in God's Word so far, is His judgment right or wrong?

Notice one more thing that people don't usually take in consideration: the timing of God's judgments and justice. Remember, the verses we read in Revelation today are previews of events yet to happen.

From what you saw today in our passages, does God execute His judgments and justice immediately, as soon as the wrong has been done?

Our study is deep. It confronts us with the truth of God's Word. Hebrews 4: 12 says

> *"For the Word of God is quick, and powerful, and sharper than any two-edged sword, piercing even to the dividing asunder of soul and spirit, and of the joints and marrow, and is a discerner of the thoughts and intents of the heart."*

Quick in this verse means living.

Are you feeling the effects of the Living Word of God as It is separating what is felt from what is spiritually discerned? Is your understanding and knowledge of the Only True God growing? How is that impacting the thoughts and intents of your heart?

📅 DAY 6

We have looked at many verses of God's Word that have shown us how He reveals Himself to us as Justice and Righteousness. Today, we are going to see what He shows us about Himself in relationship to Truth.

Begin with a time of prayer: talk to God about where you are in your heart, how you feel about Him and all the things you are learning about Him. Ask Him to help you see Him as He really is: the Only True God.

Read the verses from God's Word printed for you below three times, once aloud.

Mark every reference to **God the Father** with a blue triangle. Include all the pronouns and synonyms.

Also, mark every reference to **Jesus** with a blue triangle with a cross in it. Don't forget pronouns and synonyms.

Mark every reference to the **Holy Spirit** with a blue cloud shape, like this:

Isaiah 65:16

That he who blesseth himself in the earth shall bless himself in the God of truth; and he that sweareth in the earth shall swear by the God of truth; because the former troubles are forgotten, and because they are hid from Mine eyes.

John 1: 14

And the Word was made flesh, and dwelt among us, (and we beheld his glory, the glory as of the only begotten of the Father,) full of grace and truth.

John 14: 6

Jesus saith unto him, I am the way, the truth, and the life: no man cometh unto the Father, but by Me.

John 17: 15-17

15 I pray not that Thou shouldest take them out of the world, but that Thou shouldest keep them from the evil.

16 They are not of the world, even as I am not of the world.

17 Sanctify them thought Thy truth: Thy Word is truth.

John 16: 13

Howbeit when he, the Spirit of truth, is come, He will guide you into all truth: for He shall not speak of Himself; but whatsoever He shall hear, that shall He speak: and He will shew you things to come.

Mark every reference to *truth* with a green **T**.

What do you learn about God the Father from your markings?

What do you learn about Jesus from marking His name?

What do you learn about the Holy Spirit from these verses?

According to these verses what place does truth have in the character of God?

On Day one this week, we saw that truth is certainty, accuracy, exactitude, something that doesn't change.

The Greek word for **truth** in the passages from John that we just read, is *aletheia*. It means truly, truth, verity, and not concealed.

Truth is a very unpopular concept in our culture today. People refuse to recognize that there can be such an absolute.

The Romans struggled with that concept also: Pilate asked Jesus "what is truth?" when he was questioning Him in John 18: 38. Pilate had just asked Jesus if He was a king. Look at what Jesus answered him:

> *"To this end was I born, and for this cause came I into the world, that I should bear witness unto the truth. Everyone that is of the truth heareth my voice." John 18: 37b*

Think about that statement.

Truth is the very basis for justice. If a witness on the witness stand in a trial does not tell the truth, exactly what he saw, the defendant could be pronounced guilty of something he did not do.

Without truth, there can be no justice.

If I tell you that I am 5 feet, 6 inches tall, and you tell me that is not true, I will get a measuring tool out and show you that I am indeed 5 feet, 6 inches tall. There has to be absolute truth. It would be complete chaos if truth was whatever someone wants to believe.

Remember my Pastor's definition of truth?

" Truth is something that can be defined as true for all people, in all places, all the time.

Truth is not defined by surroundings, times, people groups or personal preferences.

Truth does not originate from within.

All truth comes from God."

Look again at John 14: 6 in our verses for today.

Jesus says "I am the …truth…".

Are you of the truth?

Do you hear His voice?

What does it mean for your day-to-day life that God is truth? How does it impact you?

📅 DAY 7

Yesterday we saw that God is truth and that all truth comes from Him.

Today, we are going to look at an essential aspect of truth that we find in God's character.

Begin by asking the Lord to help you to:

> *"Study to shew thyself approved unto God, a workman that needeth not to be ashamed, rightly dividing the Word of truth."*
> *2 Timothy 2: 15*

Read the following set of verses three times, once aloud, and mark every reference to *the LORD* with a blue triangle including all the pronouns.

Psalm 119: 89-91

89 For ever, O LORD, Thy Word is settled in heaven.
90 Thy faithfulness is unto all generations: Thou hast established the earth, and it abideth.
91 They continue this day according to Thine ordinances.: for all are Thy servants.

Psalm 102: 25-27

25 Of old Thou hast laid the foundation of the earth: and the heavens are the work of Thy hands.
26 They shall perish, but Thou shalt endure: yea, all of them shall wax old like a garment; as a vesture shalt Thou change them, and they shall be changed:
27 But Thou art the same, and Thy years shall have no end.

Psalm 33: 11

The counsel of the LORD standeth for ever, the thoughts of His heart to all generations.

Hebrews 13: 7-8

7 Remember them which have the rule over you, who have spoken unto you the Word of God: whose faith follow, considering the end of their conversation.
8 Jesus Christ the same yesterday, and to day, and for ever.

Mark the reference to *Jesus* with a blue triangle with a cross in it.

Underline every reference to time with a yellow line, such as ***all generations, this day***, etc.

What do you learn about the Lord, God, from these verses and your markings?

From what these verses tell us, will the truth of God's Word ever change?

Our culture changes all the time, new discoveries are made every day, people change their minds regularly.
Does God change? Does His counsel or His mind change? How do you know?

What do you learn about Jesus Christ in our last verse?

The fact that God does not change is essential to the fact that He is truth. Would truth be truth if it changed with the times, the personalities, or the circumstances?

God is immutable: that means that He never changes neither can He be made to change.

The Bible is the Word of God: It will never change either.

How does this foundational fact help you in a practical way in your day-to-day circumstances?

Spend some time thinking about all that we have studied this week and all that we have learned about God.

Talk to God about how you feel about Him. He has spoken to you through His Word. He wants to hear from you.

📅 WEEK 6

THE ONLY TRUE

God is Love

*"And this is life eternal, that they might know Thee
the Only True God, and Jesus Christ, Whom Thou hast sent."
John 17: 3*

We have studied many passages of God's Word in the past five chapters, and we have started to get to know God as He reveals Himself to us in His Word.

We are in this study so that we might know the Only True God personally and Jesus Christ Whom He has sent. This is eternal life.

It is good for us to remember where we started and why we are doing this.

We have begun to see that the Only True God is eternal; He has always been and will always exist.

He created everything and everyone.

He rules over all with complete and total sovereignty.

He knows all.

He is everywhere all the time.

He can do anything and everything He wants to.

He is Righteous; He can do no wrong.

He is Just; He cannot be unfair or unequal.

He is Truth, completely exact and totally accurate.

And He never changes.

What an awesome God!

It can be intimidating to realize the majesty and grandeur of God. We feel insignificant, minuscule, even expendable, as we consider Who He is.

But no! We are not insignificant to Him at all!

In this chapter we are going to see the value and worth He gives us as we study another amazing facet of God's character: love.

Prepare your heart: you might fall in love in a way you never imagined before!

 DAY 1

Begin with prayer.

The first time that we find any reference to love coming from God, in His Word, is in Deuteronomy 4.

The love of God mentioned there is for the people that He chose to be His people, Israel.

We can learn much from looking at several passages of the Old Testament, in which God assures Israel of His love for them.

Read the following passages three times, once aloud. Mark every reference to the **LORD** with a blue triangle including the pronouns.

Deuteronomy 4: 31, 37

31 (For the LORD thy God is a merciful God;) He will not forsake thee, neither destroy thee, nor forget the covenant of thy fathers which He sware unto them.

...

37 And because He loved thy fathers, therefore He chose their seed after them, and brought thee out in His sight with His mighty power out of Egypt;

Deuteronomy 7: 6-10

6 For thou art an holy people unto the LORD thy God: the LORD thy God hath chosen thee to be a special people unto Himself, above all people that are on the face of the earth.

7 The LORD did not set His love upon you, nor choose you, because ye were more in number than any people;

8 But because the LORD loved you, and because He would keep the oath which He had sworn unto your fathers, hath the LORD brought you out with a mighty hand, and redeemed you out of the house of bondmen, from the hand of Pharaoh king of Egypt.

9 Know therefore that the Lord thy God, He is God, the faithful God, which keepeth covenant and mercy with them that love Him and keep His commandments to a thousand generations;

10 And repayeth them that hate Him to their face, to destroy them: He will not be slack to Him that hateth Him, He will repay him to his face.

Deuteronomy 10: 15

Only the Lord had a delight in thy fathers to love them, and He chose their seed after them, even you above all people, as it is this day.

Hosea 11: 1

When Israel was a child, then I loved him, and called my son out of Egypt.

Jeremiah 31: 1-3

1 At the same time, saith the Lord, will I be the God of all the families of Israel, and they shall be my people.

2 Thus saith the Lord, The people which were left of the sword found grace in the wilderness; even Israel, when I went to cause him to rest.

3 The Lord hath appeared of old unto me, saying, Yea, I have loved thee with an everlasting love: therefore with lovingkindness have I drawn thee.

Mark every reference to ***love*** and ***lovingkindness*** with a red heart, like this:

What do you learn from marking these two words?

There is a contrast between v.9 and v.10 in the passage from Deuteronomy 7. Write down what is being contrasted with what:

Write what you learn about God in the verses from Deuteronomy.

Is God fair in stating this? Why or why not? Base your answer on what we have learned about Who God is in our study so far.

In Deuteronomy, God declares His love for Israel. He chooses to love Israel just because He wants to, not because of who they are or what they have done. Neither is He choosing to love them because of what He will get in return for His love.

When we read through the Old Testament, we see how the people of Israel betray His love with their stubborn and rebellious hearts. They disregard His love, guidance and protection, and run after other gods.

The verses from Hosea and Jeremiah show how God feels about them after all of their betrayals.

What do you learn about God's relationship with the people that He chose to love from those verses?

Is there a time limit to His love for them?

 DAY 2

"My soul followeth hard after Thee; Thy right hand upholdeth me."
Psalm 63: 8

As you begin today's study with prayer, ask the Lord to help you follow hard after Him.

Today, we will look at how God reveals His love to us in the New Testament of His Word.

The first time we read about God's love in the New Testament is in John 3. This is where we discover how deep and how far the love of God reaches.

Read the following verses three times, once aloud. Mark every reference to **God** with a blue triangle and every reference to ***Jesus Christ*** with a blue triangle with a cross inside of it. Don't forget the pronouns.

John 3: 16-17

16 For God so loved the world, that He gave His only begotten Son, that whosoever believeth in Him should not perish, but have everlasting life.
17 For God sent not His Son into the world to condemn the world; but that the world through Him might be saved.

Romans 5: 6-10

6 For when we were yet without strength, in due time Christ died for the ungodly.
7 For scarcely for a righteous man will one die: yet peradventure for a good man some would even dare to die.
8 But God commendeth His love toward us, in that, while we were yet sinners, Christ died for us.
9 Much more then, being now justified by His blood, we shall be saved from wrath though Him.

10 For if, when we were ennemies, we were reconciled to God by the death of His Son, much more, being reconciled, we shall be saved by His life.

Ephesians 2: 4-5

4 But God, Who is rich in mercy, for His great love wherewith He loved us,
5 Even when we were dead in sins, hath quickened us together with Christ, (by grace are ye saved;)

Mark every reference to **love** with a red heart as you did yesterday.

Write everything you learn about God from marking **God** in theses verses.

What do you learn about **Jesus Christ** in the verses we are studying today?

According to these verses, what is the proof or the evidence that God loves you? In other words what did God and Jesus do that shows their love for us?

Look for every word that includes people like *the world*, *whosoever*, *we*, *us*, and circle them.

What were we like when God chose to love us?

What does that tell us about God?

So, do we need to be good for God to love us? Do we need to clean up our lives or "walk the straight and narrow" so that God will love us? How do we know?

Close your study time today by talking to the Lord about how you feel about what you have studied today… He's waiting for you, longing for you to share your heart with Him.

DAY 3

We need another day to see how God has chosen to love us, just because!

Start as we always should: talk to Him in prayer; ask Him to help you see and comprehend what He wants so much for us to know about him.

Read the following verses three times, once aloud, as you think about what they are saying to us.

1 John 3: 1

Behold, what manner of love the Father hath bestowed upon us, that we should be called the sons of God: therefore the world knoweth us not, because it knew Him not.

1 John 4: 9-10, 16, 19

9 In this was manifested the love of God toward us, because that God sent His only begotten Son into the world, that we might live through Him.
10 Herein is love, not that we loved God, but that He loved us, and sent His Son to be the propitiation for our sins.
...
16 And we have known and believed the love that God hath to us. God is love; and he that dwelleth in love dwelleth in God, and God in him.
...
19 We love Him, because He first loved us.

Mark every reference to **God** with a blue triangle and every reference to Jesus Christ, His **Son**, with a blue triangle with a cross inside it. Make sure you mark the synonyms and pronouns like **Father**.

Mark the word, **love,** with a red heart in these verses, every time you see it.

Make a list of everything you learn in these verses about **God**. This may seem tedious and repetitious, but when we persevere in studying this way, we find out that the Holy Spirit speaks to our hearts and shows us things we would never see if we didn't take the time to do this. As you see theses things and as you begin to make applications to your own life, write down these Life Lessons anywhere in the blank parts of this study. You will be so glad when you can read back over them and remember the precious truths God taught you about Himself and how they apply to your life.

About **God**:
1 John 3:1 He bestows upon us a love that causes us to be called His sons
The world doesn't know Him

Now make a list of everything you learn about His **Son**, Jesus-Christ:

Even though some of these observations might cross over, make a list of everything you learn from marking **love**:

Now that you have completed these keyword lists, let's ask and answer some W's and H questions.

How did God show His love for us?

Why can we love God?

Now these are deeper questions to think about and answer: according to these verses, what is love? What does love do for the loved one?

Are you amazed? Is your heart filled with awe as you think about all this? Talk to God about it.

 # DAY 4

Today, we are going to look at a very special, unique relationship and the love that flows in it.

Though it is difficult for our finite minds to comprehend the concept of God being three persons, yet one God, we can see in His Word that His love for His Son, the Lord Jesus Christ, is unlike any other.

Begin this time of studying by going before the Throne of Grace and asking God to open the eyes of your understanding.

The verses we will focus on today are in the Gospel of John. The Gospel of John presents the Lord Jesus Christ as the Son of God. The verses below describe the love God has for His Son.

Read them three times, once aloud, and mark the key words we have been focusing on: **God**, **Son/Jesus-Christ**, **love,** as you have been marking them so far. Make sure to get all the pronouns and synonyms too.

John 3: 35-36

35 The Father loveth the Son, and hath given all things into His hand.
36 He that believeth on the Son hath everlasting life: and he that believeth not the Son shall not see life; but the wrath of God abideth on him.

John 17: 22-26

22 And the glory which Thou gavest me I have given them; that they may be one, even as We are One:
23 I in them, and Thou in me, that they may be made perfect in one; and that the world may know that Thou hast sent me, and hast loved them, as Thou hast loved Me.
24 Father, I will that they also, whom Thou hast given Me, be with Me where I am; that they may behold My glory, which Thou hast given Me: for Thou lovedst Me before the foundation of the world.

25 O Righteous Father, the world hath not known Thee: but I have known Thee, and these have known that Thou hast sent Me.
26 And I have declared unto them Thy Name, and will declare it: that the love wherewith Thou hast loved Me may be in them, and I in them.

In the first passage from John 3 we see God the Father, the Son, and us. We see that the Father loves the Son, and that we are divided into two categories: those who believe on the Son, and those who do not.

In the second passage, John 17, Jesus is praying, talking to God, His Father, about His relationship with those of us who believe.

Write down everything you learn about **God** in these verses.

(Pay close attention to all the pronouns: don't miss what each key word you mark is telling us about God. For example, in v. 22 we can mark Thou because it stands for God, and what we learn here is that He gave glory to Jesus Christ. Be faithful in observing the details, and soon you will see wondrous things, that are not seen when doing a simple reading.)

What do you learn from marking the references to the **Son, Jesus-Christ**?

It may seem like you are writing the same things again, but go ahead and list below what you learn from marking **loveth, loved, lovedst**, and **love**:

(Remember, the Holy Spirit is guiding you, teaching you...sit patiently; listen closely to the still, small voice)

From what you have observed, what does God's love do for Jesus-Christ, His Son?

In John 17: 24 & 26 it is evident that Jesus is very confident and sure of His Father's love for Him. What does Jesus want to do with the love of His Father? Look at v. 26.

The love of God for Jesus, His Son, described in these verses, expresses the essential nature and character of God.

From what you have seen so far, what kind of love is God's love for His Son?

We have more to observe, but this is enough for today. Meditate on these observations, and ask God to continue to show Himself to you through the pages of His Word.

 DAY 5

We finished our study yesterday by thinking about what kind of love is God's love.

We know there are many different kinds of love: a mother's love for her child is different from the love between two friends.

The love between brothers is different from the love of a man for a woman.

We also know that when we say we love ice-cream, it is not the same meaning as when we say, "I love you," to someone.

There are actually five different words in the Greek language that are translated love (or desire) in English: *Epithumia, Eros, Storge, Phileo, and Agape.*

- *Epithumia* means longing for, desiring, craving, lust
- *Eros* means passionate, sentimental, romantic yearning to unite with and possess
- *Storge* means a natural family love, tender affection, a comfortable sense of belonging
- *Phileo* means to have affection for someone, to be fond of
- *Agape* means affectionate regard, goodwill, benevolence, wanting what is best for the one loved at any cost.

With that in mind, begin with prayer asking the Lord to help you grow in understanding His love.

Read the following verses three times and once aloud.

1 John 4: 7-8

7 Beloved, let us love one another: for love is of God; and every one that loveth is born of God, and knoweth God.
8 He that loveth not knoweth not God; for God is love.

Romans 8: 31-32, 35, 37-39

31 What shall we then say to these things? If God be for us, who can be against us?

32 He that spared not His own Son, but delivered Him up for us all, how shall He not with Him also freely give us all things?

...

35 Who shall separate us from the love of Christ? shall tribulation, or distress, or persecution, or famine, or nakedness, or peril, or sword?

...

37 Nay, in all these things we are more than conquerors through Him that loved us.

38 For I am persuaded, that neither death, nor life, nor angels, nor principalities, nor powers, nor things present, nor things to come,

39 Nor height, nor depth, nor any other creature, shall be able to separate us from the love of God, which is in Christ Jesus our Lord.

Go back over the verses you just read and mark every reference to **God** with a blue triangle. Mark every reference to **Jesus Christ, God's Son** with a blue triangle with a cross in it. Circle every word that refers to **believers**, including the pronouns **us** and **we**, draw a red heart over every **love** or **loved.**

According to 1 John 4: 7 where does love come from?

In *Vine's Expository Dictionary* we read, "Love can be known only from the actions is prompts." [2]

Using your keyword markings **God** and **love**, make a list of all the actions that come from God's love in the verses you just read. (Hint: look at at God's actions in v.32).

2| W. E. Vine, *Vine's Expository Dictionary of Old and New Testament Words,* (Old Tappan, NJ, Fleming H. Revell Company, 1981), 21 of Volume 3: Lo-Ser

Without looking up which greek word for love is used in the verses we are studying today, what kind of love do you see revealed by God's actions?

List what you learn from marking the references to those who belong to Christ. Write only what you learn in these verses.

What is the constant that will always be there for all believers, no matter what happens in their lives?

When we experience hardships, trials, and struggles in our lives, the pain can lead us to wonder if God really loves us. How can knowing the truths that we just saw in the verses above help us in these difficult times?

In Romans 8: 37 we see the answer to the question in Romans 8: 35. It shows us what we can be in all these difficulties. Write down what v. 37 says that we can be in "all these things":

How can we be what this states? The answer is at the end of v. 37: don't miss it! Is it by our own strength? By pulling ourselves up "by our boot straps"?

This is only the beginning of looking what kind of love God has and is. Is it a love that removes all trials, difficulties and pain?

That will be enough to think about for today. Tell the Lord how you feel about what you have seen today.

📅 DAY 6

Today, we are going to study a chapter of *the Bible*, God's Word, that has been called, "The Love Chapter," by many. 1 Corinthians 13 is the best description of the love of God.

Begin with prayer. Ask God to help you understand His attribute of love better than you ever have.

Read the following passage three times, once aloud.

You will not see the word, love, in this passage, but instead, you will see that the main key repeated word, is ***charity***. In the greek text, the language in which the New Testament was written, the word that was translated ***charity*** is *agape,* one of the five words translated love in english.

Yesterday, we read in 1 John 4: 8 ***"God is love"***.

The greek word for love, in 1 John 4: 8 is also agape.
As you read the following passage, keep in mind that ***charity*** is *agape* love.

1 Corinthians 13

1 Though I speak with the tongues of men and of angels, and have not charity, I am become as sounding brass, or a tinkling cymbal.
2 And though I have the gift of prophecy, and understand all mysteries, and all knowledge; and though I have all faith, so that I could remove mountains, and have not charity, I am nothing.
3 And though I bestow all my goods to feed the poor, and though I give my body to be burned, and have not charity, it profiteth me nothing.
4 Charity suffereth long, and is kind; charity envieth not; charity vaunteth not itself, is not puffed up,
5 Doth not behave itself unseemly, seeketh not her own, is not easily provoked, thinketh no evil;
6 Rejoiceth not in iniquity, but rejoiceth in the truth;

7 Beareth all things, believeth all things, hopeth all things, endureth all things.

8 Charity never faileth: but whether there be prophecies, they shall fail; whether there be tongues, they shall cease; whether there be knowledge, it shall vanish away.

9 For we know in part, and we prophesy in part.

10 But when that which is perfect is come, then that which is in part shall be done away.

11 When I was a child, I spake as a child, I understood as a child, I thought as child: but when I became a man, I put away childish things.

12 For now we see through a glass, darkly; but then face to face: now I know in part; but then shall I know even as also I am known.

13 And now abideth faith, hope, charity, these three; but the greatest of these is charity.

Since *charity* in this passage means agape love, mark every occurrence of the word *charity* with a red heart over it, just like you marked love previously.

List everything you learn about the characteristics of *agape* love from marking the word *charity*:

You will notice that there are several comparisons and contrasts in this chapter.

In the first three verses we see comparisons when contrasted with charity.

Complete the chart started for you below:

Verse	Characteristic/Gift/Ability	Contrast	Comparison
v. 1	Speaking with tongues of men Speaking with tongues of angels	charity	Sounding brass Tinkling cymbal
v. 2			
v. 3			

Now, look at v.8-13 and notice the many contrasts that the apostle Paul gives us to think about. They are all indicated by the word **but**. Whenever we see the word, **but**, there is usually a contrast to take note of.

Use the table below to see what is contrasted with what:

Verse	What	But	What
v. 8	*Charity never fails*	*but*	*prophecies will fail* *tongues will cease* *knowledge will vanish away*
v. 9-10			
v. 11			
v. 12			
v. 13			

What do you think the apostle Paul was trying to communicate? What is the most important point of this passage? (There is no right or wrong answer to this question; write what the Holy Spirit is showing you. He is our Master Teacher, and He knows what He wants you to see.)

Conclude your study today with a time of praise and worship: how can we not be in awe of the Only True God's amazing love?

 # DAY 7

"For God so loved the world, that He gave His only begotten Son, that whosoever believeth in Him should not perish, but have everlasting life." John 3: 16

The **Only True God** loves us, every single one of us. Each one of us is included in **whosoever.**

Such extreme, intense love demands a response.

Are we going to love Him?

Or, are we going to tell Him that we are not interested and walk away from the **Only True God**?

"Examine yourselves, whether ye be in the faith; prove your own selves." 2 Corinthians 13: 5a

Our study today will be about the response of those who choose to love the **Only True God**.

Begin with prayer. Ask the Lord to search your heart and show you what He wants you to see.

Read the following passages three times, and one of those times read them aloud.

1 John 5: 1-3

1 Whosoever believeth that Jesus is the Christ is born of God: and everyone that loveth Him that begat loveth Him also that is begotten of Him.

2 By this we know that we love the children of God, when we love God, and keep His commandments.

3 For this is the love of God, that we keep His commandments: and His commandments are not grievous.

1 John 3: 14-18, 23

14 We know that we have passed from death unto life, because we love the brethren. He that loveth not his brother abideth in death.

15 Whosoever hateth his brother is a murderer: and ye know that no murderer hath eternal life abiding in him.

16 Hereby perceive we the love of God, because He laid down His life for us: and we ought to lay down our lives for the brethren.

17 But whoso hath this world's good, and seeth his brother have need, and shutteth up his bowels of compassion from him, how dwelleth the love of God in him?

18 My little children, let us not love in word, neither in tongue; but in deed and in truth.

…

23 And this is His commandment, That we should believe on the name of His Son Jesus Christ, and love one another, as He gave us commandment.

John 13: 34-35

34 A new commandment I give unto you, That ye love one another; as I have loved you, that ye also love one another.

35 By this shall all men know that ye are my disciples, if ye have love one to another.

Go back over the passages now to mark the key words that we will focus on today. Circle every reference to people, such as **_whosoever_, _we_, _us_, _you_, _men_**, etc… Include the pronouns for these as well.

Draw a red heart over the word, **_love,_** in all its forms.

There is another very obvious key words that is repeated in all three of these passages. Did you see it? If you did, go ahead and mark it with your own color or symbol.

What do you learn from marking the references to people?

What does the love of God produce in the hearts of those who choose to love Him?

According to these verses, what should be the characteristics of our lives if we choose to respond to the love of God by loving Him?

The key word repeated in all three of our passages today is *commandment*. If you didn't already mark it in our verses, do so now with your own color or symbol.

What do you learn from marking *commandment*?

What will be the result of keeping God's commandments, according to these verses?

It is time to reflect upon all the wonderful truths we have studied this week.

Have you perceived the love of God? Have you seen His love in how He laid down His life for us in the person of Jesus Christ His Son?

What is the response of your heart? Examine yourself. Are you in the faith? How do you know?

If you love the Lord, the **_Only True God_**, and you have kept His commandment by believing on the Name of His Son, Jesus Christ, accepting Him as your Savior, you can take this time now to thank Him and worship Him for His great love.

If you want to respond to God's amazing gift of His love and of His Son's death on the cross to pay for your sin, simply acknowledge your sin to Him. Tell Him that you understand that you cannot pay for your own sin, and that you accept His free gift of salvation by believing on the Name of His Son Jesus Christ as your Savior.

God will pour out His love in your heart through the Holy Spirit, and you will have eternal life with Him, and so much more! You will be a new person, with a hunger and thirst to know Him more and to keep His commandments. You will live to please Him,

> *"And the peace of God, that passeth all understanding, shall keep your hearts and minds through Christ Jesus." Philippians 4: 7*

📅 WEEK 7

THE ONLY TRUE

God is Holy

For the past six weeks, we have been studying to know the Only True God as He reveals Himself in His Word, *the Bible*. As we begin the final week and chapter of this study, are you beginning to see that a lifetime will not be enough to fully know the Only True God? He is truly infinite, and indeed, so much more than we can completely comprehend. That is probably why the Apostle Paul prayed for the Colossians in this way:

> *"For this cause we also, since the day we heard it, do not cease to pray for you, and to desire that ye might be filled with the knowledge of His will in all wisdom and spiritual understanding; That ye might walk worthy of the Lord unto all pleasing, being fruitful in every good work, and increasing in the knowledge of God;" Colossians 1: 9-10*

Though this is the last chapter of this study, pray that it will be a springboard into a lifetime of increasing in the knowledge of our awesome God!

This is a summary of what we have seen in the last six weeks:

- God has always been and will always be: **He is Eternal.**
- God created everything that exists and has existed: **He is the Creator.**
- God is in complete control of everything and everyone: **He is Sovereign.**
- God can do anything He wants to: **He is Ominipotent.**
- God is present everywhere: **He is Omnipresent.**
- God knows everything: **He is Omniscient.**
- God always does what is right: **He is Righteous.**
- God is always totally fair: **He is Just.**
- God is absolute accuracy: **He is Truth.**
- God loves and does what is best for all of mankind at any cost: **He is Love.**

There is one more very important truth about Whom the Only True God is. It is probably the most misunderstood truth about Him.

Some try to ignore it; others try to change what it means or how it affects our relationship with Him.

Yet, if we miss the significance of this truth about God, we will not be able to know the Only True God, because this attribute is a part of all of God's attributes.

This truth qualifies and delineates all of the truths we have studied about God.

God is Holy.

We all desperately need to learn and understand what that means because He wants us to be holy as He is holy.

> *"But as He which hath called you is holy, so be ye holy in all manner of conversation;*
> *Because it is written, Be ye holy; for I am holy." 1 Peter 1: 15-16*

📅 DAY 1

As you begin today's study with prayer, try kneeling before the Lord in humble acknowledgement of all that He has shown you about Himself so far.

Ask him to prepare your heart so that you will increase in the knowledge of Him today.

Today, we are going to look at a lot of verses from God's Word because this will show us how gently, patiently, precisely and amazingly God reveals His holiness to us.

When we study a topic in Scripture, the first time it is mentioned is a very important place to start.

So, let's begin by reading the following passage from Exodus 3. This is the first time in God's Word that the word, **_holy,_** occurs.

Make sure you read this passage three times, and one of those times aloud.

Mark every reference to **_God_** with a blue triangle. Mark every occurrence of the word, **_holy,_** with a cloud, like this:

Exodus 3: 1-6

1 Now Moses kept the flock of Jethro his father in law, the priest of Midian: and he led the flock to the backside of the desert, and came to the mountain of God, even to Horeb.

2 And the angel of the Lord appeared unto him in a flame of fire out of the midst of a bush: and he looked, and behold, the bush burned with fire, and the bush was not consumed.

3 And Moses said, I will now turn aside, and see this great sight, why the bush is not burnt.

4 And when the Lord saw that he turned aside to see, God called unto him out of the midst of the bush, and said, Moses, Moses. And he said, Here am I.

5 And He said, Draw not nigh hither: put off thy shoes from off thy feet, for the place whereon thou standest is holy ground.
6 Moreover He said, I am the God of thy father, the God of Abraham, the God of Isaac, and the God of Jacob. And Moses hid his face: for he was afraid to look upon God.

Write down what you learn about *God* in these verses:

Now let's ask several W and H questions. Do your best to answer strictly with what the text mentions.

Where was this taking place?

Why did Moses turn aside?

What did Moses say about what he saw?

What did God tell Moses to do?

Why did God tell him to do this? (Make sure to answer only according to what you read in the verses. Don't interpret or analyze yet. For now, we are in the observation stage.)

What did Moses do when God revealed Himself to Moses?

Why did he do that?

Finally, what does God call *holy* in this first occurrence of this word?

This is the first time we encounter the word, *holy,* in the Word of God, and it is not used to describe God Himself, but it is used to describe something related to God.

Keeping that in mind, look up the following verses and passages writing down what is described as *holy.*

■ Exodus 12: 12-17

■ Exodus 15: 1, 9-13

■ Exodus 16: 4-5, 22-23, 20: 8

■ Exodus 19: 4-6

■ Exodus 22: 31

■ Exodus 25: 8, 26: 1, 33-34

■ Exodus 28: 1- 30: 38 (This will be a long reading; be diligent and patient to read it all. Allow the Holy Spirit to show you what God is doing through all the minute details that He tells Moses to do. You only need to write down what items are described as **holy** as you read these long chapters.)

Do you begin to see what God is doing? Do you see the way in which He is introducing us to His glorious holiness?

His ways are so precise and purposeful, yet so gentle and patiently loving.

Wherever you are in your understanding of Him, take some time now to close your time of study by talking with Him. He is there, waiting for you.

📅 DAY 2

Begin your study time today as we always should: asking God for His transforming power to renew your mind as you look into His Word to learn of Him.

So far, we have seen God introduce us to His holiness by first showing us that anything and anyone that relates to Him must be holy.

Our study was all in the second book of God's Word, *Exodus*.

Today, we are going to be in the third book of God's Word, *Leviticus*, where we see how God presents Himself to His people Israel, the people He chose to be set apart, a holy nation,

"a peculiar treasure unto Me above all people" Exodus 19: 5

Read the following verses three times, once aloud, and mark every occurrence of **God** with your blue triangle including all the synonyms and pronouns that refer to Him.

Leviticus 11: 44-45

44 For I am the LORD your God: ye shall therefore sanctify yourselves, and ye shall be holy; for I am holy: neither shall ye defile yourselves with any manner of creeping thing that creepeth upon the earth.
45 For I am the LORD that bringeth you up out of the land of Egypt, to be your God: ye shall therefore be holy, for I am holy.

Leviticus 19: 2

Speak unto all the congregation of the children of Israel, and say unto them, Ye shall be holy: for I the LORD your God am holy.

Leviticus 20: 26

And ye shall be holy unto Me: for I the LORD am holy, and have severed you from other people, that ye should be mine.

Leviticus 21: 8

Thou shalt sanctify him therefore: for he offereth the bread of thy God: he shall be holy unto thee: for I the LORD, which sanctify you, am holy.

Leviticus 22: 31-33

31 Therefore shall ye keep my commandments, and do them: I am the LORD.
32 Neither shall ye profane My holy Name: but I will be hallowed among the children of Israel: I am the LORD which hallow you,
33 That brought you out of the land of Egypt, to be your God: I am the LORD.

Make a list of everything these verses tell us about **God.**

Reading these verses, especially aloud, you inevitably see and hear the word, *holy,* repeated throughout. Go back over the verses and mark every occurrence of the word, *holy*. Include the synonyms that you notice.

List what you notice about *holy*: (always remember to ask the 5 Ws and an H)

Who is *holy*?

Who is commanded to be *holy*?

Who hallows/sanctifies those who are commanded to be *holy*?

With what is *holy* contrasted?

Did you notice the *therefore* and *for*? What are they there for? What is the conclusion being made?

At this point, we need to do a Word Study. We need to dig deeper to find out just what *holy* means. It is obviously very important to God, and about Him. We must understand the meaning.

In order to do a Word Study, we need to start with the original word used in these verses. A *Strong's Exhaustive Concordance* and a Hebrew Dictionary are the tools we need to do this.

Using *Strong's Concordance,* we find that *holy,* in the verses we have been studying, is word #6944.

That Hebrew word is *qodesh.*

In the Hebrew and Chaldee Dictionary that is included in the back of *Strong's Concordance,* we read that *qodesh* means: consecrated, dedicated, hallowed, holiness, holy, saint, and sanctuary.

In the *Theological Wordbook of the Old Testament,* we find further information about what *holy* means: *qodesh* means apartness, holiness, sacredness, hallowed, and holy. The following are quotes from the *Theological Wordbook of the Old Testament*:

> "The noun *qodesh* connotes the concept of "holiness", i.e. the essential nature of that which belongs to the sphere of the sacred and which is thus distinct from the common or profane." [3]

> "But the biblical viewpoint would refer the holiness of God not only to the mystery of His power, but also to His character as totally good and entirely without evil." [4]

3| R.Laird Harris, Gleason L. Archer, Jr., Bruce K. Waltke, *Theological Workbook of the Old Testament,* (Chicago, Moody Publishers, 1980) 787
4| R.Laird Harris, Gleason L. Archer, Jr., Bruce K. Waltke, 787

"Holiness is separate from all that is sinful and profane." [5]

"It is unthinkable that a holy God could condone sin; such a concept would involve a diffusion of the sacred and profane, thus destroying the nature of holiness." [6]

Using these descriptions, how would you define what God means when He says "I am holy"?

Can God tolerate sin?

We studied the love of God, and found that He is love. Does that mean that He can accept sin in us?

> *"Behold the LORD's hand is not shortened, that it cannot save;*
> *neither His ear heavy, that it cannot hear:*
> *But your iniquities have separated between you and your God,*
> *and your sins have hid His face from You, that He will not hear."*
> *Isaiah 59: 1-2*

Think about these truths, and let the Holy Spirit show you what the Only True Holy God has done, out of His infinite love, so that our sin would no longer separate us from Him.

5| R.Laird Harris, Gleason L. Archer, Jr., Bruce K. Waltke, *Theological Workbook of the Old Testament*, (Chicago, Moody Publishers, 1980) 788
6| R.Laird Harris, Gleason L. Archer, Jr., Bruce K. Waltke, 788

📅 DAY 3

Studying the holiness of God is intense.

It inevitably confronts us with both what we are not, and with the awesomeness of God. It can actually give us a sense of hopelessness: how can we ever be holy as He is holy?

This brings to mind the words of a beautiful song , "Yet not I, but through Christ in me". Those words are based on Philippians 4: 13:

> *"I can do all things through Christ which strengtheneth me."*

Begin with prayer. Ask God to continue to help you learn of Him.

When we do a Word Study, we gain insight by looking at the meaning of the synonyms and the antonyms of the word.

Look back over the verses we studied yesterday and see if you notice any synonyms and antonyms (or contrasts) to the word *holy*.

They may be in a different grammatical form such as a verb. Look for any word that is used to convey the same concept and any word that seems to make a contrast with *holy*.

Look specifically at these verses:

Leviticus 11: 44

For I am the LORD your God: ye shall therefore sanctify yourselves, and ye shall be holy; for I am holy: neither shall ye defile yourselves with any manner of creeping thing that creepeth upon the earth.

Leviticus 21: 8

Thou shalt sanctify him therefore: for he offereth the bread of thy God: he shall be holy unto thee: for I the LORD, which sanctify you, am holy.

Leviticus 22: 32

Neither shall ye profane My holy Name: but I will be hallowed among the children of Israel: I am the LORD which hallow you,

Ezekiel 22: 26

Her priests have violated My law, and have profaned Mine holy things: they have put no difference between the holy and profane, neither have they shewed difference between the unclean and the clean, and have hid their eyes from My sabbaths, and I am profaned among them.

Did you notice **sanctify, hallowed** and **clean**? Those are synonyms.
Did you notice **defile, profane** and **unclean**? Those are antonyms.

■ Sanctify

The Hebrew word for sanctify is *qadash*. It means to be clean, to consecrate, to dedicate, to purify.

■ Hallowed

This is the same word in Hebrew as **sanctify,** *qadash,* which means clean, consecrated, dedicated.

■ Clean

The Hebrew word for clean is *tabor,* which means pure.

■ Defile

This is the word, *tame,* in Hebrew, and it means: to be foul, contaminated, to be unclean.

■ Profane

This is the Hebrew word, *chalal.* It means to bore, to wound, to break, to pollute, to prostitute, to stain.

■ Unclean

The Hebrew word for unclean is *tame.* It means foul, defiled, polluted.

If you didn't have a concordance or a Hebrew word dictionary to use, you could do an internet search to find out what *holy* means.

Here is what you would find at synomyms.com:

holy (adjective)
Perfect or flawless.

Antonyms:
damaged, faulty, imperfect, defective, flawed
Synonyms:
flawless, perfect, faultless

Do these synonyms and antonyms help you better understand what God means when He says, "*I am holy*"?

Write down what you have learned about the seriousness of God's holiness:

When we study God's Word, it is very helpful to look at other verses that contain the same word or topic that we are studying. This is called cross-referencing. Doing this allows Scripture to interpret Scripture.

We should always look at all the cross-references we can find before going to see what others have written in commentaries. Commentaries are man's words and man's interpretation of what God says in His Word.

God's Words are living: as we read the whole counsel of God's Word and meditate, we think about what we read, and the Holy Spirit shows us what God means.

Begin with the following verses. Think about what they are telling us about holiness.

Leviticus 10: 8-11

8 And the Lord spake unto Aaron, saying,

9 Do not drink wine nor strong drink, thou, nor thy sons with thee, when ye go into the tabernacle of the congregation, lest ye die: it shall be a statute for ever throughout your generations:

10 And that ye may put difference between the holy and unholy, and between unclean and clean;

11 And that ye may teach the children of Israel all the statutes which the Lord hath spoken unto them by the hand of Moses.

Hebrews 7: 26

(this is describing the Lord Jesus Christ)

For such an High Priest became us, Who is holy, harmless, undefiled, separate from sinners, and made higher than the heavens;

What do these verses say about what ***holy*** means?

There is still more to search in order to better understand God' s holiness.

Close your time of study by asking the Lord to help you understand more and better about His holiness.

📅 DAY 4

Begin with prayer.

There are over 500 occurrences of the word, *holy,* in God's Word, and over 40 occurrences of the word, *holiness*.

By comparison, there are 442 occurrences of the word, *love,* in *the Bible*.

God obviously wants us to understand His holiness.

Further study of cross-references will be our focus today.

If we can understand God's holiness, and why He wants us to be holy, our perspective will change. That change will direct our hearts in the choices that we make.

Read each of the following verses and mark the word, *holy,* as you did before.

Then answer the questions below each verse using strictly what the verse(s) tell us.

Deuteronomy 23: 14

> For the Lord thy God walketh in the midst of thy camp, to deliver thee, and to give up thine enemies before thee; therefore shall thy camp be holy: that He see no unclean thing in thee, and turn away from thee.

Why should the camp be holy?

What would keep the camp from being holy?

What will God do if the camp is not holy?

Joshua 24:19

And Joshua said unto the people, Ye cannot serve the Lord: for He is an holy God; He is a jealous God; He will not forgive your transgressions nor your sins.

Can God look the other way when we sin? Why?

Psalm 15

1 Lord, who shall abide in Thy tabernacle? who shall dwell in Thy holy hill?
2 He that walketh uprightly, and worketh righteousness, and speaketh the truth in his heart.
3 He that backbiteth not with his tongue, nor doth evil to his neighbour, nor taketh up a reproach against his neighbour.
4 In whose eyes a vile person is contemned; but he honoreth them that fear the Lord. He that sweareth to his own hurt and changeth not.
5 He that putteth not out his money to usury, nor taketh reward against the innocent. He that doth these things shall never be moved.

This Psalm describes what God means by being holy. You can make a list of the characteristics of holiness from this Psalm. Complete the list started for you below:

Being holy is:
- *walking uprightly: living right*
- *working righteousness: doing what is right*
- *speaking the truth in my heart: thinking right*

Psalm 145: 17

The LORD is righteous in all His ways, and holy in all His works.

What seems to go hand in hand with holiness?

Ephesians 5: 25-27

25 Christ also loved the church, and gave Himself for it;
26 That He might sanctify and cleanse it with the washing of water by the Word,
27 That He might present it to Himself a glorious church, not having spot, or wrinkle, or any such thing; but that it should be holy and without blemish.

Notice the contrast in v. 27: the word "but" tells us something is being contrasted. This contrast helps us see a little more of what holy means.

Write what the glorious church is not, and the contrast of what it should be:

It is so sad to hear people all around us use the word "holy" as part of an interjection, without realizing what they are saying.

Holiness is such and important attribute of the Only True God.

It should not be a word that we use lightly or flippantly.

In conclusion of today's study, gather your thoughts and write down what you would answer if someone came to you and asked you, "What does it mean that God is holy?"

 # DAY 5

Begin today's study with prayer as we always should.

Today, we need to look at an attribute of God that is not easy to face, but it is an essential attribute that is directly related to God's holiness.

Because God is holy, pure, undefiled, He cannot accept, tolerate or ignore sin in any way, shape or form. No matter how much He loves, He is holy first and foremost: without sin.

Think of a surgeon who is about to open up a patient's body to remove something or correct something. The area he is going to cut is thoroughly disinfected and cleansed with powerful bacteria-killing products so that the surgeon does not introduce bacteria into the patient's body.

The surgeon scrubs his hands, arms, fingers, nails very rigorously before putting on two sets of gloves that have been sterilized. The area he is going to cut is draped with a sterile towel that has a small opening for where the incision will be made. Everyone that is going to assist the surgeon is gowned and masked with sterile gowns and masks; they have rigorously scrubbed also and put on two layers of sterile gloves.

All this is very strictly regulated and done so that bacteria is not allowed into the patient's body.

If one person enters the operating room without a mask on, or if someone, who is not wearing sterile gloves and gown, touches the sterile field where the surgeon is about to make the incision, the field is considered contaminated, and the surgery is cancelled. The risk of contaminating the patient with bacteria cannot be tolerated.

We are all very thankful that medical professionals have understood the danger of contamination and how to prevent it. No one tolerates shortcuts to these very tedious procedures because they can mean life or death for the patient.

Sin is like bacteria.

Sin contaminates, and it causes death.

It cannot be tolerated by a Holy God.

He loves us. We saw how much He loves us in our last chapter. He does not want us to die.

> *"The Lord is not slack concerning His promise, as some men count slackness; but is long-suffering to us-ward, not willing that any should perish, but that all should come to repentance."*
> *2 Peter 3: 9*

It is because of sin that we see the wrath and jealousy of God.

God must judge sin, or He would not be holy.

God tells us in His Word that there is a day of wrath coming, in which He will reveal His judgment for sin.

Read the following verses three times, once aloud, and mark every reference to **God** with a blue triangle including the pronouns that refer to Him.

John 3: 36

He that believeth on the Son hath everlasting life: and he that believeth not the Son shall not see life; but the wrath of God abideth on him.

Romans 1: 16-19

16 For I am not ashamed of the gospel of Christ: for it is the power of God unto salvation to every one that believeth; to the Jew first, and also to the Greek.

17 For therein is the righteousness of God revealed from faith to faith: as it is written, The just shall live by faith.

18 For the wrath of God is revealed from heaven against all ungodliness and unrighteousness of men, who hold the truth in unrighteousness;

19 Because that which may be known of God is manifest in them; for God hath shewed it unto them.

Romans 2: 2-8

2 But we are sure that the judgment of God is according to truth against them which commit such things.

3 And thinkest thou this, O man, that judges them which do such things, and doest the same, that thou shalt escape the judgment of God?

4 Or despisest thou the riches of His goodness and forbearance and long-suffering; not knowing that the goodness of God leadeth thee to repentance?

5 But after thy hardness and impenitent heart treasurest up unto thyself wrath against the day of wrath and revelation of the righteous judgment of God;

6 Who will render to every man according to his deeds:

7 To them who by patient continuance in well doing seek for glory and honour and immortality, eternal life:

8 But unto them that are contentious, and do not obey the truth, but obey unrighteousness, indignation and wrath,

9 Tribulation and anguish, upon every soul of man that doeth evil, of the Jew first, and also of the Gentile;

Romans 5: 8-9

8 But God commendeth His love toward us, in that, while we were yet sinners, Christ died for us.

9 Much more then, being now justified by His blood, we shall be saved from wrath through Him.

Ephesians 5: 3-6

3 But fornication, and all uncleanness, or covetousness, let it not be once named among you, as becometh saints;

4 Neither filthiness, nor foolish talking, nor jesting, which are not convenient: but rather giving of thanks.

5 For this ye know, that no whoremonger, nor unclean person, nor covetous man, who is an idolater, hath any inheritance in the kingdom of Christ and of God.

6 Let no man deceive you with vain words: for because of these things cometh the wrath of God upon the children of disobedience.

1 Thessalonians 1: 9-10

9 For they themselves shew of us what manner of entering in we had unto you, and how ye turned to God from idols to serve the living and true God;
10 And to wait for His Son from heaven, whom He raised from the dead, even Jesus, which delivered us from the wrath to come.

Go back over the verses you just read, and mark the words, *wrath* and *judgment,* in a color of your choice.

List everything you learn about *God* from these verses. Look at your blue triangles and note what each occurrence tells us about God:

Using only what we read in today's verses, write everything you see about about *wrath* and *judgment.*

Whose wrath is it?

What causes the wrath? Why is there wrath?

What are those, who will suffer from this wrath called?

How can we be saved from this wrath?

If you look carefully, you will notice two opposite sets of behaviors and attitudes of the heart in these verses; they are in contrast. Use the table below to list those behaviors and attitudes as you look for them in each passage:

Will Escape God's Wrath	Will Receive God's Wrath

Close your study by asking God to show you the relationship between His wrath and His holiness. Write what He shows you.

 # DAY 6

"Who is like unto Thee, O LORD, among the gods? who is like Thee, glorious in holiness, fearful in praises, doing wonders?"
Exodus 15: 11

Think about all that we have studied so far as you begin with prayer.

Ask the Lord to help you see Him for Who He really is.

When we see God, the Only True God, as He reveals Himself to us in His Word, something happens to us within our hearts.

Read the following passage of Scripture three times, slowly, and once aloud.

Isaiah 6: 1-5

1 In the year that king Uzziah died I saw also the Lord sitting upon a throne, high and lifted up, and His train filled the temple.
2 Above it stood the seraphims: each one had six wings; with twain he covered his face, and with twain he covered his feet, and with twain he did fly.
3 And one cried unto another, and said, Holy, holy, holy, is the LORD of hosts: the whole earth is full of His glory.
4 And the posts of the door moved at the voice of him that cried, and the house was filled with smoke.
5 Then said I, Woe is me! for I am undone; because I am a man of unclean lips, and I dwell in the midst of a people of unclean lips: for mine eyes have seen the King, the LORD of hosts.

Go back over the verses you just read, and mark every reference to God, which are *the LORD* and the pronouns referring to Him, with a blue triangle.

Then, mark every reference to Isaiah, the one who was inspired by the Holy Spirit to write these verses, in a color or shape of your choice.

Using your blue triangle markings, make a list of what you learn about the Lord from this passage:

How did Isaiah feel as a result of seeing the Lord?

What did Isaiah become painfully aware of, as he saw the Lord?

How about you?
You have worked diligently and faithfully to complete this study so far.
You have seen the Lord through His Word.
How do you see yourself now that you see the Only True God?

Does understanding the holiness of God make you want to change anything about the way you live the life that He has given you to live?

📅 DAY 7

Begin today with thanking the Lord for how He has spoken to you through His Word as you have diligently studied and learned of Him.

Spend time listening to His still small voice.

Enjoy the calm quietness of being still and knowing that He is God.

Ask Him to continue to deepen the relationship you have with Him through today's study.

Read the following verses three times, once aloud, and mark every reference to *God* including the pronouns.

2 Corinthians 6: 14, 16-18; 7: 1

14 Be not unequally yoked together with unbelievers: for what fellowship hath righteousness with unrighteousness? And what communion hath light with darkness?

...

16 And what agreement hath the temple of God with idols? for ye are the temple of the living God; as God hath said, I will dwell in them, and walk in them; and I will be their God, and they shall be My people.

17 Wherefore come out from among them, and be ye separate, saith the Lord, and touch not the unclean thing; and I will receive you,

18 And will be a Father unto you, and ye shall be my sons and daughters, saith the Lord Almighty.

7: 1 Having therefore these promises, dearly beloved, let us cleanse ourselves from all filthiness of the flesh and spirit, perfecting holiness in the fear of God.

Ephesians 4: 17-24

17 This I say therefore, and testify in the Lord, that ye henceforth walk not as other Gentiles walk, in the vanity of their mind,

18 Having the understanding darkened, being alienated from the life of God through the ignorance that is in them, because of the blindness of their heart:

19 Who being past feeling have given themselves over unto lasciviousness, to work all uncleanness with greediness.

20 But ye have not so learned Christ;

21 If so be that ye have heard Him, and have been taught by Him, as the truth is in Jesus:

22 That ye put off concerning the former conversation the old man, which is corrupt according to the deceitful lusts;

23 And be renewed in the spirit of your mind;

24 And that ye put on the new man, which after God is created in righteousness and true holiness.

1 Thessalonians 4: 7

For God hath not called us unto uncleanness, but unto holiness.

1 Peter 1: 14-16

14 As obedient children, not fashioning yourselves according to the former lusts in your ignorance:

15 But as He which hath called you is holy, so be ye holy in all manner of conversation;

16 Because it is written, Be ye holy; for I am holy.

Go back over the verses above and mark the words, ***holiness*** and ***holy***, as you did before.

Make a list of what you learn from marking holiness and holy:

(it is started for you)

2 Cor. 7: 1 • *holiness is to be perfected*

           • *we must perfect holiness because we fear God*

           • *we perfect holiness when we cleanse ourselves from all filthiness of flesh and spirit*

There are repeated contrasts in these four passages. Did you see them? Each of these passages mention opposites ; some are easy to see because of the word, **but,** between them.

Look for these contrasts and note what is contrasted with what in the chart below:

(It is started for you)

Reference	Description	Contrast
2 Cor. 6: 14	*righteousness*	*unrighteousness*
2 Cor. 6: 14	*light*	*darkness*
2 Cor. 7: 1	*filthiness of the flesh and spirit*	

Don't worry about "getting it right"; just continually ask the Holy Spirit to show you what He wants you to see. He will. What He shows you is the right answer.

According to 1 Thessalonians 4: 7, what is God's calling for believers, those who have learned, heard and been taught by Jesus Christ, His Son?

What do these passages show believers about how to fulfill God's calling?

According to 1 Peter 1: 15-16, is fulfilling God's calling optional for believers?

You marked every reference to **God** when you were reading these passages. Now, look at each marking and list what each one tells you about God:

(it is started for you)

2 Cor. 6: 16 • *God has a temple*

• *God is living*

• *believers are His temple*

• *God wants to dwell in believers*

Did you see the longing of God's heart?

This longing of the heart of God is a theme that runs throughout His Word. From Genesis to Revelation we see God's deepest longing. Right after creation when God was walking in the garden where He had placed man and his wife, He is calling and looking for them. In Leviticus He gives His people the instructions of the law to bridge the gulf of separation that sin imposed. In Revelation the future new earth and new heaven are revealed, a place where God can be with men. This is God's deepest longing:

"And I will set My tabernacle among you: and My soul shall not abhor you.
And I will walk among you, and will be your God, and ye shall be My people." Leviticus 26: 11-12

"And I heard a great voice out of heaven saying, Behold, the tabernacle of God is with men, and He will dwell with them, and they shall be His people, and God Himself shall be with them, and be their God." Revelation 21: 3

The Only True God wants to be your God.

He wants you to be His. He wants to walk with you and dwell with you. Are you ready and willing to respond to His call to be holy?

Examine your heart, your life. Is there anything you need to change to respond to God's call to holiness?

KNOW

THE ONLY TRUE

GOD

THIS IS ETERNAL LIFE

"This is life eternal, that they might know Thee the Only True God" John 17: 3

This was our purpose for the past seven weeks.

It has been a long and detailed study and we have looked at many passages of God's Word.

To refresh our memory on the main truths we have seen, here is a summary:

- God has always been and will always be: **He is Eternal.**
- God created everything that exists and has existed: **He is the Creator.**
- God is in complete control of everything and everyone: **He is Sovereign.**
- God can do anything He wants to: **He is Omnipotent.**
- God is present everywhere: **He is Omnipresent.**
- God knows everything: **He is Omniscient.**
- God always does what is right: **He is Righteous.**
- God is always and completely fair: **He is Just.**
- God is absolute accuracy: **He is Truth.**
- God loves and does what is best for all of mankind at any cost: **He is Love.**
- God is totally good, perfect, entirely without evil: **He is Holy.**

This list is awe-inspiring.

This is the Only True God.

This is what He tells us about Himself in His Word, *the Bible.*

Pause and reflect upon this.
Read it over several times; ask yourself: do I believe this?
Do I live in the light of these truths?

This is what God wants us to know about Him. Does this make you want to adjust the way you go about life?

In the book of Amos, we find God showing the prophet Amos a plumbline. He tells Amos,

> *"Behold, I will set a plumbline in the midst of my people"*
> *Amos 7: 8*

The Word of God, *the Bible*, is that plumbline: it shows us the truth; what is correct and straight; what is accurate.

Are we willing to line up our beliefs and thoughts about God according to the plumbline of His Word?

Think about all that you have learned from His Word about Who the Only True God is.

What is your heart's desire now that you see Who He is?